Esports and the Media

This book takes a multidisciplinary approach to the question of esports and their role in society. A diverse group of authors tackle the impact of esports and the ways in which it has grown within the entertainment industry around the world.

Chapters offer a coherent response to the following questions: What role do esports play in the entertainment industry? What communication skills can be learned through esports? What do the media gain from broadcasting esports? What is the relationship between social networks and esports? What are the main marketing strategies used in esports? What effect does communicative globalization have on the development of esports? What is the relationship between merchandising and esports? What do communication experts think about esports?

Offering clear insights into this rapidly developing area, this volume will be of great interest to scholars, students, and anyone working in game studies, new media, leisure, sport studies, communication studies, transmedia literacy, and digital culture.

Angel Torres-Toukoumidis completed his PhD in Communication under the research line 'Media Literacy' at the universities of Huelva, Seville, Málaga, and Cádiz. He is Principal Investigator of the first university games laboratory in Ecuador (GAMELAB-UPS http:// gamelab.ups.edu.ec/). He is also currently Lecturer at the Universidad Politécnica Salesiana, Ecuador.

Routledge Focus on Digital Media and Culture

For more information about this series, please visit: https://www.routledge.com/Routledge-Studies-in-Genocide-and-Crimes-against-Humanity/book-series/RSGCH

Esports and the Media

Challenges and Expectations in a Multi-Screen Society

Edited by
Angel Torres-Toukoumidis

Routledge
Taylor & Francis Group
London and New York

First published 2023
by Routledge
4 Park Square, Milton Park, Abingdon, Oxon OX14 4RN

and by Routledge
605 Third Avenue, New York, NY 10158

Routledge is an imprint of the Taylor & Francis Group, an informa business

This book has been made open access with generous funds from Gamelab-UPS, Research Group, and Universidad Politécnica Salesiana, Ecuador.

British Library Cataloguing-in-Publication Data
A catalogue record for this book is available from the British Library

Library of Congress Cataloging-in-Publication Data
A catalog record has been requested for this book

ISBN: 9781032222653 (hbk)
ISBN: 9781032226781 (pbk)
ISBN: 9781003273691 (ebk)

DOI: 10.4324/9781003273691

Contents

Figures

Tables

Contributors

Bruno Duarte Abreu Freitas holds a PhD in Experimental Sciences and Technology (with a specialization in Marketing) from UVic-UCC, Spain. He is interested in marketing and entrepreneurship and has published several papers on the esports market.

Daniel Barredo-Ibáñez is Associate Professor at Universidad del Rosario, Colombia, as well as Invited Researcher at Fudan University, China. He holds a PhD in Journalism from Universidad de Málaga, Spain. He is Senior Researcher, the highest qualification obtainable from the regulatory body in Colombia. His research interests are digital media, social media, and social appropriation of knowledge.

Gabriela Borges holds a PhD in Communication and Semiotics from the Catholic University of São Paulo. She is Lecturer at the Education and Communication School as well as Researcher at CIAC (Arts and Communication Research Centre), University of Algarve, Portugal. She is Coordinator of the Audiovisual Quality Observatory (UFJF) and Alfamed Brasil (Euro-American Inter-university Research Network on Media Literacy for Citizenship).

Mari Carmen Caldeiro Pedreira holds a PhD in Communication and Education. She is Teacher at University of Santiago de Compostela (Spain), Lecturer at different Spanish universities, and Teacher at Latin American universities (Chile and Ecuador). She is Teacher at University of Distance Education and Researcher at Center for Higher Education Studies (Czech Republic). She is also Member of advisory board and Scientific Reviewer to national and international journals.

Luis Ever Caro-Lazos is Director of Research and Postgraduate Studies at the Faculty of Accounting and Administration, Universidad Autónoma de Chihuahua, Mexico. He holds a PhD in Administration from Universidad Autónoma de Chihuahua. He belongs to the

National System of Researchers (SNI-Candidate) in Mexico (Consejo Nacional de Ciencia y Tecnología) and has published several journal articles and book chapters.

Ruth S. Contreras-Espinosa holds a PhD in Multimedia, and has been involved in a set of projects within the EU sector (H2020) and in projects funded by the government of Spain. She has authored papers on gamification, serious games, and esports.

Susana Costa is a PhD student in Digital Media Art (Universidade do Algarve and Universidade Aberta), with a research grant from the Foundation for Science and Technology. She has integrated working groups in the areas of education and technology and has published articles in national and international journals as well as book chapters.

Andrea De-Santis is Professor and Director of the Communication and Social Communication degree programs, and of the Master's degree in Communication and Sports Journalism at UPS. He is a member of the research group in Communication, Education and Environment (GICEA) at UPS.

José Ángel Garfias Frías is Professor at the National Autonomous University of Mexico. He holds a PhD in Political and Social Sciences, and is National Researcher at Level 1 in the National Council of Science and Technology, Mexico. He is coordinator of La Finisterra, a research group on videogames, animation, and other creative industries.

Erika Lucía González Carrión holds a PhD from the Interuniversity Doctoral Program in Communication in Media Literacy, University of Huelva, Spain. She has a Master's degree in Communication and Audiovisual Education from the University of Huelva as well as a Bachelor's Degree in Social Communication and in Educational Sciences with a major in English Language from Loja, Ecuador.

Sonia Esther González-Moreno is Coordinator of Research and Postgraduate Studies at the Faculty of Accounting and Administration, Universidad Autónoma de Chihuahua, Mexico. She holds a PhD in Education, Arts, and Humanities from UACH. She belongs to the National System of Researchers (SNI-1) in Mexico (CONACYT) and has published several journal articles and book chapters.

Paulo Carlos López-López is Lecturer at the Faculty of Political Science of the Universidade de Santiago de Compostela, Spain, and holds a PhD in Political Communication. He is member of the Equipo de Investigaciones Políticas. He is Editor of several scientific journals and has more than 100 publications. His research interests are political communication, social media, political participation, and technology.

Roberto Alejandro López Novelo is Research Professor at the Faculty of Communication, Universidad Anáhuac, Mexico. He holds a PhD in Political and Social Sciences from the National Autonomous University of Mexico. He is Member of the National System of Researchers of the National Council for Science and Technology, Mexico, and his research lines are social capital, entertainment, creative industries, and digital culture.

Isidro Marín-Gutiérrez holds a PhD in Social Anthropology from the University of Granada (2008). He also studied Sociology at the University of Granada (1999) and completed his third cycle advanced studies in Granada in the doctoral program "Health, Anthropology and History" (2000–2002). He holds a Master's degree in Opinion Studies (2002) and has worked at the University of Huelva, Spain (2004–2014) and at Universidad Técnica Particular de Loja, Ecuador (2013–2021). He is currently working as Assistant Professor Doctor at the University of Seville, Spain.

Luis Fernando Morales Morante is Coordinator of the official Master's Degree in Strategic Planning in Advertising and Public Relations, and Professor at the Department of Advertising, Public Relations and Audiovisual Communication at Universitat Autónoma de Barcelona, Spain. He has collaborated in research, development, and innovation projects within the framework of the Horizon 2020 program.

Jesús Manuel Palma-Ruiz is Full Professor at the Faculty of Accounting and Administration, Universidad Autónoma de Chihuahua, Mexico. He holds a PhD in Business & Entrepreneurial Management from the University of Cantabria, Spain. He belongs to the National System of Researchers (SNI-1) in Mexico (CONACYT), has published in indexed journals, and has co-edited international books.

Daiana Sigiliano is a PhD student in Communication at the Federal University of Juiz de Fora (UFJF), Brazil, and holds an MA degree in Communication from UFJF. She is Researcher at the Ibero-American Observatory of Television Fiction (Obitel – Brasil), member of Alfamed Brasil (Euro-American inter-university research network on media literacy for citizenship) and of the Audiovisual Quality Observatory.

Angel Torres-Toukoumidis completed his PhD in Communication under the research line "Media Literacy" at the universities of Huelva, Seville, Málaga, and Cádiz. He is Principal Investigator of the first university games laboratory in Ecuador (GAMELAB-UPS http://gamelab.ups.edu.ec/). He is also currently Lecturer at the Universidad Politécnica Salesiana, Ecuador.

Javier F. A. Vega Ramírez is an academic at the Institute of Educational Sciences, and Associate Researcher at GAMELab, Salesian Polytechnic University of Ecuador. His research interests are educational policies, pedagogical narratives, religious education, and the use of videogames as a teaching resource.

Acknowledgments

I thank Gamelab-UPS, Research Group, and Universidad Politécnica Salesiana, Ecuador for all their support.

Part I
Overview

1 E-sports in the Entertainment Industry

Overview

Andrea De-Santis and Luis Fernando Morales Morante

The debate is open. In the last decade the opinions and criteria in favor of its recognition as a sport discipline has meant the upcoming inclusion in the 2022 Asian Games, the development of an official event around Paris 2024 Olympic Games and a possible inclusion in the Los Angeles 2028 Olympic Games (Álvarez, 2019). E-sports have been subjected to an analysis on the relevance of their conceptual definition by the academic community and experts, in terms of whether their characteristics agree or are comparable with the characteristics of other sports. Specifically, critics of e-sports emphasize the absence of the physicality that defines the semantic nature of the term and its relationship with physical exercise (Coakley, 2008). Undoubtedly, like chess, e-sports require fine motor skills that allow the fast and precise use of muscles (Haibach et al., 2017; Jenny et al., 2016), and involve a brain effort capable of assuming 20% of a person's energy, even more so when he or she is a professional (Álvarez, 2019). Also, they are characterized by the competitive level of their events, the formal organization of leagues and collegiate bodies, as well as their operation in relation to an industrial, commercial and economic system very similar to traditional sports (Hou et al., 2020). Finally, it is not an individual sport, and its projection to competition has resulted in the highest revenues for professional players, organizations and sponsors (Newzoo, 2021).

Regarding the second question, Hamari and Sjöblom (2017, p. 122) define e-sports as "competitive video game structured around leagues and tournaments"; the concept is clarifying, although a bit reductive. The team in charge of e-sports at Newzoo further specifies the concept as "professional or semi-professional competitive gaming in an organized format (tournament or league) with a specific goal/prize, such as winning a championship title or prize money" (Newzoo, 2021, p. 6). The current and visible reality of the big leagues and their millionaire prizes, advertising, live-streaming events, the mythification of players

DOI: 10.4324/9781003273691-2

and fan communities make e-sports a great spectacle with global projection and converging interests of different sectors of society. Its popularity and the attention it has generated in different players is the result of its innate capacity to evolve with information and communication technologies (ICTs) and, above all, the synergy it has generated with the media. The first chapter of this book offers a reconstruction of the history of e-sports and its evolution toward the current recognition and performance in the world of sports and entertainment as a product of the relationship with the mass media and the audience, a growth that converges in the challenges of a sport discipline and its market.

The origins of e-sports and its relationship with the media

The e-sports industry was formally institutionalized at the beginning of the new millennium and has gained scientific interest in the last decade (Hou et al., 2020; Schubert et al., 2016). Its origins date back to the 1980s and the emergence of competitive video game events. Game journalist Tristan Donovan (2010) points to the Intergalactic Space Warfare Olympics held in 1972 at the Massachusetts Institute of Technology (MIT) as the first electronic gaming competition in history. According to Borowy and Jin (2013) the first official event was the tournament organized by the American company Atari in New York, which was able to gather more than 10,000 Space Invaders players (Polsson, 2012). The event had an important media coverage and, therefore, according to the authors, it originated the relationship between the world of video game competitions and the mass media. In fact, among the following events organized by Atari and other companies (Kent, 2001), there were initiatives promoted by television channels such as Starcade (1982–1984) and That's incredible! (1980–1984), in which players compete in front of the audience.

In their detailed historical reconstruction, Borowy and Jin (2013) show how the influence of the renewed and innovative media staging of the 1984 Olympic Games held in Los Angeles has revolutionized the way of conceiving the staging of sporting spectacle worldwide. In the same year, the Video Game Masters Tournament, the most prestigious national competition in the United States at the time, was held and, by coincidence, the Olympic escalation of e-sports could finish and there is a possibility that the Olympic escalation of e-sports will culminate in their inclusion precisely in the city of Los Angeles in 2028 (Álvarez, 2019). Whatever their destiny, the visibility that the media offer to video game competitions and the effect of their commercial proactivity will define the e-sports industry after 40 years.

Undoubtedly, the forming of a gamer culture contributes significantly to shaping e-sports. The boom in the interactive electronic games market benefited from the then consolidated where the main consumers of video games gathered (Burnham, 2001). The experience accumulated by younger generations has defined the characteristics of a gaming culture stimulated by the beginning of the computer age and a greater compulsion toward new forms of entertainment (Borowy and Jin, 2013). E-sports result from these cultural practices generated by the relation to the conceptual models of sport and media in which the experience can be both physical and non-physical. According to Toffler (1970), an experiential product can be constituted in live or simulated environments, and e-sports represent a synthesis of these two elements since they are live events that occur by simulated computerization, where the media is the space of competition (Borowy & Jin, 2013).

The key role of the gamer culture audience and the commercialization of video game competitions change the way both the product and the experience are consumed, stimulating the use of video game tournaments and events as complementary initiatives to other types of events. The powerful attraction of competition and the recognition of achievements by the winners increase the motivation of players and spectators, highlighting another characteristic of the sport. The appearance in 1981 of a media specialized in the collection and dissemination of information about tournaments, players and their results, such as the Official Scoreboard for Electronic Entertainment (Twin Galaxies), not only marks another historical fact symbolizing the importance of the media in the evolution of e-sports, but also evidences the growing interest of the audience. *Time* magazine's 1981 interview of teenager Steve Juraszek for his record in a 16-hour game (Kent, 2001), *Life* magazine's feature on the Twin Galaxies arcade and its star players (Burnham, 2001) and the inclusion of the best player of the year in the 1985 Guinness Sports Record are examples of the contribution of the media toward the professionalization of e-sports and its players, in addition to its appeal to the public and the interest of other industries in the entertainment industry (Kent, 2001).

The boom of the e-sports industry and its consolidation in the entertainment industry

Because of the Internet, the '90s were the correct scenario for the consolidation of e-sports. The possibility of transferring the gaming context to the digital world opened the doors for future competitions between professional and amateur gamers. Technological convergence stimulated big tournaments and events with more recognition by society. Companies such as Nintendo and Blizzard Entertainment made their mark on the scene, with the former organizing two world championships (1990 and 1994) and the latter launching StarCraft (1998), which is considered the first e-sports game after *Wired* magazine in 1993 had recognized the free software Netrek as the first online video game sport (Kelly, 1993). The American industry is the first to show a real boom thanks to the staging of events capable of offering competitions, contests and online video games at the same time, as well as a space to promote business relationships with professionals and companies in the sector such as the Electronic Entertainment Expo (E3), a specialized event held in the United States since 1995, which allows access to the general public since 2017.[1]

The new millennium is the beginning of the e-sports industry. In 2000, the expansion of this sporting activity began with the creation of the World Cyber Gamer, the international competition considered as the true Olympics of e-sports (Hutchins & Rowe, 2012). In the same year, the first official international tournament of StarCraft was also held (Karhulahti, 2017), a real-time strategy video game that only two years after its release could boast the title of best seller in 1998 with more than 1.5 million copies worldwide, and 9.5 million in the following ten years (Olsen, 2007). The greatest acceptance for this video game (4.5 million copies of the total) is registered in South Korea, currently considered the homeland of modern e-sports (Taylor, 2012), a country in which professional players are influencers (Jin, 2010), and there is an institutionalized association dedicated to the regulation of all matters related to e-sports such as certification and organization of competitions (Jonasson & Thiborg, 2010). The success achieved by StarCraft places it as a reference game in the world of e-sports in terms of defining the requirements and standards for the future development of games at the center of the e-contest, such as League of Legends (LOL), Defender of the Anciest 2 (DOTA2) and Fortnite, which are among the most popular (Goal, 2021; Hou et al., 2020; Marca, 2021; Newzoo, 2021).

The current industry leader is LOL, launched in 2009 by Riot Games, and it was able to supplant the supremacy of StarCraft in just two years because of the first world tournament conducted by it (Waigh, 2021). It is a video game typical of the multiplayer online battle arena (MOBA) genre, a subgenre of real-time strategy video games that originated as a component for StarCraft and was subsequently positioned as a genre of its own, being successfully exploited by LOL. It allows team play while the individuality of each player can be maintained thanks to the network connection, which has registered record numbers for the industry, connecting millions of players around the world at the same time (Tejera, 2013). In 2021, the LOL world championship registered 174.82 million hours of viewing by the multiplatform audience over the 134 hours of competition broadcast, approximately more than 67 million views with respect to the International 10 (TI10) of DOTA2, the second event with the highest views. This result is more relevant if considering that six of the events that complete the top ten of the most watched e-sports competitions in 2021 are LOL competitions, including three editions of the mobile version of the game (Table 1.1).

The leadership of MOBA games is evident with eight games out of ten in the ranking, while the remaining two are from the shooter genre. LOL and DOTA2 take the lion's share of the current industry revenues by capturing the largest audience and the highest economic values in terms of sponsorships. This means more significant prizes and economic profits for players and professional teams in these leagues that

Table 1.1 Most watched e-sport competences in 2021

No.	Competence	Game	Views	Broadcasted hours
1	League of Legends Worlds Championship 2021	League of Legends	174,820.000	134
2	Dota 2: The International 10	DOTA2	107,230.000	125
3	Mobile Legends: MPL ID Temporada 8	League of Legends	76,940.000	172
4	Counter-Strike: Stockholm PGL Major	Counter-Strike: Global Offensive	71,260.000	120
5	League of Legends: Spring LCK Split	League of Legends	67,640.000	290
6	Mobile Legends: Worldwide championship M3	League of Legends	62,610.000	103
7	League of Legends: MSI 2021	League of Legends	61,180.000	86
8	League of Legends: Summer LCK	League of Legends	60,520.000	295
9	Mobile Legends: MPL ID 7 Season	League of Legends	54,290.000	169
10	Valorant Champions 2021	Valorant	46,040.000	98

Source: Based on Borisov (2021)

receive salaries for their sporting activity that can reach up to 10,000 euros per month (Waigh, 2021).

Therefore, the e-sports industry is the result of different factors and interests linked to its relationship with the media. Its electronic identity projected and enhanced by the computer era, the commoditization of players' experiences, the transmission of competitions and the institutionalization process driven by media coverage and the growing interest of audiences created an industry capable of being compared to the sports disciplines that are part of the major leagues of the sports and entertainment industry.

Evolution and trends in the relationship between media and e-sports

The current status as a sport activity in the formalization and developing industry process drives e-sports toward a new change in the rules and in the way of presenting its value to the different stakeholders, repeating the history that began in the 1980s. As at that time, its relationship with the traditional media and the multi-platform and hyper-connected digital ecosystem of the information society (De-Santis-Piras & Morales Morante, 2019) assumes different roles, drawing a scenario of opportunities and threats for the future of e-sports. The perfect example occurred during the COVID-19 pandemic, with a young industry that has suffered economic losses caused by the cancellation of events and the reinvention of tournaments, but that has once again been able to take advantage of its privileged connection with electronics and ICT, capturing part of the audiences of traditional sports totally blocked by prevention and biosecurity measures (Gando, 2021). There are some trends that should have the attention of experts and stakeholders in the sector, as well as be the subject of further study by the academic community. The following is a description of those that are more significant because of the interpretation of the results recorded so far by e-sports, and their possible projection toward their development.

Increased newsworthiness for the world of e-sports

The broadcasting of the first e-sports tournaments, the production of specific programs on the subject and live competitions have contributed to the creation of a specific audience composed mainly of teenagers and young people (Hou et al., 2020). The increased interest and recognition generated by official competitions and gaming leagues have captured the attention of journalists and the media, expanding the range of opportunities for the general public to approach the world of e-sports. In the early '80s, a significant part in the media attacked e-sports for their negative influence on the youth (Kardefelt-Winther, 2014). Gradually, the increased awareness and the relevance assumed by the increase of its audience motivated greater media coverage and interest deepening about this activity and its protagonists, including their careers and private lives (Hivoorde & Pot, 2016). The role of the media is to act as a bridge between the world of e-sports and part of an audience who lack information and knowledge to understand and appreciate it. Regarding the national and regional realities that have experienced a greater development of the industry, there is evidence of a central role of the media in the dissemination and greater acceptance of e-sports among citizens. In China, the traditional media have shifted their narrative toward increasingly positive positions over 17 years of coverage (Hou et al., 2020); the centrality of South Korea in the e-sports market has been aided by the creation of thematic channels with 24 hours of programming 7 days a week, promoting the expansion of a modern gamer culture in which players and professionals are socially recognized and have influence (Jin, 2010).

Role of live broadcasting platforms

According to projections made by Newzoo (2021), the global audience for live streaming of e-sports in 2021 reached 728.8 million with a growth rate of 10% over 2020, and with an increasing projection for 2024. The lock-in conditions determined by governments around the globe because of the pandemic have produced an increase in the adoption of streaming systems for e-sports tournaments and competitions (Newzoo, 2021). Undoubtedly, the trend toward the use of platforms for live streaming has been observed since 2011 with the creation of Justin.tv, better known by the renewed (2014) brand of Twitch.tv, the emergence of YouTube live accessible to the entire public since 2013 (Pires & Simon, 2015) and the creation of specialized services such as Huya.tv in 2012 and Douyu.tv in 2014 (Hou et al., 2020), until the most recent Facebook Gaming (2018).

These platforms revolutionize the e-sports industry by giving a greater role to the main stakeholder, i.e., the audience. It is mainly about participating in the game, being part of the sporting spectacle with more protagonism than a simple spectator, commenting on the plays in real time, giving or receiving suggestions, creating a market for fans that results in consumers of the experiential product predicted by Toffler (1970), and shaped both by its physical dimension and by the experience, emotion and its memory for which the e-sports consumer is willing to pay.

Professionalization of e-sports in the entertainment industry

Since the first tournaments and championships, e-sports have gradually changed the way we understand both the competition and the contenders (Hilvoorde & Pot, 2016). The number of spectators that multiplied in and from arcades to the multiplatform media has meant a greater professionalization of gamers and a greater interest in their achievements, careers and personal lives (Hou et al., 2020). Awards make the gamer's career attractive, and the increasing fame and profitability give a prestigious status to this new professional sports figure. One of the oldest examples of professionalization is represented by the first official US video game team formed in 1980 with a marketing function for expanding the video game market to new audiences (Borowy & Jin, 2013). Also, the inclusion of gamers with the best scores in the 1986 Guinness Sports Records and the media coverage in magazines and newspapers has contributed to the institutionalization of the professional figure of the e-sportsman. One player identified as a pioneer gamer is the American Billy Mitchell, who in 1985 registered six Guinness records in arcade video games (Goal, 2021). Today, international championships of the most popular games award million-dollar prizes and players are superstars followed by millions of fans who praise or criticize them for their sporting performances. The group dimension has gained its place on the scene thanks to MOBA games that require the interoperability of coordinated and trained players. Each team specializes in one or more games; among the most famous are the Faze Clan (USA), Team Secret (Russia), Fnatic (UK) and Team Liquid, which has been active since 2000 with its participation in the first StarCraft tournament (Brand, 2019). The level of status offered by media visibility increases the public image of gamers just like in the case of stars in other sports and in the film and entertainment industry, with significant influence on national youth culture (Jin, 2010).

Development of online communities on streaming platforms

The interactivity of digital platforms and the live broadcasting of events have fostered greater participation of e-sports players and audiences. Likewise, the use of platforms such as Twitch has motivated the creation of online communities of fans who interact with each other and with players and industry experts (Sjöblom & Hamari, 2017). The proximity offered by direct communication with the champions and idols of the various games has allowed the spread of gamer culture and the impulse toward the specialization of news coverage because of the evolution in the relationship between e-sports and media. On streaming platforms, strategies and criteria about the game and competitions are exchanged, focusing the attention of a group of consumers with low loyalty rates compared to the entertainment market, such as young people. Digital communities are generally composed of fans, mostly men and young (Hou et al., 2020). They prefer games of skill and strategy, attend face-to-face events and live streaming of competitions and 59% of them dedicate more than 15 hours a week to the game and participate in at least five events, with 60% of them under 18 years old (Macey et al., 2021). Undoubtedly, the adult-age audience has increased in the last decade, occupying a good part of the total audience (Deloitte, 2018). The existence of specialized thematic communities and specific interaction channels produces a network of influences in which players, media and institutions can modify the perception of e-sports, as well as provide a greater knowledge of consumers and their behavior.

Challenges of e-sports in the multi-screen society

E-sports are now the boom. Although the pandemic has hindered the conduction of international and face-to-face competitions in physical spaces, e-sports have taken advantage of the opportunities offered by an emerging scenario by transferring their competitions to the virtual environment whenever possible, being an entertainment alternative due to the suspension of competitions in almost all traditional sports. In a multi-screen society through which people access a hyper-connected world, e-sports seem to overcome challenges with the same value as their characters in the simulated or fantasy world of games. However, the e-sports industry demands the connection of concrete and organized responses.

The main challenge is to continue to maintain the interest in e-sports, as well as the effort toward a better understanding and appreciation by the public. Human beings learn from their environment based on direct experience or through other human beings who provide information and its possible interpretation. The public is not yet familiar with the world of e-sports, which is why the work of professionals and the media is essential, which must break their preconceptions and aim for greater specialization in the specific field. This is also a challenge for the profession of sports journalists and an opportunity for specialization in favor of both the e-sports industry and the professional category.

The ability of e-sports to take advantage of the continuous technological development does not only encompass the characteristics of the "game", as its value lies in the synthesis managed with the experience lived by the player or spectator, involving its stakeholders in the process, from sponsors as the driving force of the industry to organizers, consumers, media and fans. In these terms, a further challenge is to constantly contribute to the improvement of game mechanics, dynamics and aesthetics (De-Santis & Armendáriz González, 2020) and to entertain the spectator, offering the possibility of exploiting technological innovation in favor of a more efficient visualization, greater interactivity and understanding of e-sports. A possible key to action is to bet on information that takes advantage of multimedia as a language to reach the public.

In fact, the decisions made by the pioneers of this industry and the current leaders have driven the emergence of new national markets and the exponential increase of consumers and operators for its proper sporting, technological and commercial development. Undoubtedly, the internationalization process of e-sports finds obstacles linked to the regulatory reality of each scenario, the lack of market regulation and the institutionalization of e-sports in different national and regional contexts (Li, 2017). The main solution identified and promoted by experts and academics points to a greater institutionalization of the system and intervention by government bodies of the different states through the creation of centralizing bodies for the policy and administration of e-sports, to regulate tournaments and intervention areas of the different actors, as well as their rights and responsibilities (Hou et al., 2020).

Finally, the growing recognition of cyber athletes is a driving factor for the development of e-sports in that it minimizes the lack of constancy of entertainment consumers, thanks to the personalization of the relationship with the players, direct contact, the mythification of the champion and his achievements, a basic element of sports that reaches a relevant media dimension.

Finally, there are negative aspects linked to the practice and consumption of e-sports that have not been studied in this chapter and should be addressed scientifically and by experts and government agencies, such as gender discrimination caused by the masculinization of e-sports, the violence contained in the games and compulsive gambling as a modern disease.

References

Álvarez, D. (2019, de enero de 3). ¿Videojuegos olímpicos?. *El País*. https:// elpais.com/deportes/2019/01/02/actualidad/1546443921_180851.html

Borisov, A. (2022, de enero de 19). Torneos de Esports más vistos de 2021. *ESPORTS CHARTS*. https://escharts.com/blog/most-watched-tournaments-2021

Borowy, M., & Jin, D. Y. (2013). Pioneering e-sport: the experience economy and the marketing of early 1980s Arcade Gaming contests. *International Journal of Communication, 7*, 2254–2274. https://doi.org/1932–8036/20130005

Burnham, V. (2001). *Supercade: a visual history of the videogame age 1971–1984*. Cambridge: MIT Press.

Coakley, J. (2008). Ethnic competition and the logic of party system transformation. European *Journal of Political Research, 47*(6), 766–793. https://doi.org/10.1111/j.1475-6765.2008.00824.x

Deloitte. (2018). ¿Cuáles son los retos de los eSports en España? https://www2.deloitte.com/es/es/pages/technology-media-and-telecommunications/articles/retos-esports-espana.html

De Santis Piras, A., & Armendáriz González, D. A. (2020). Jugando a la Pandemia entre los newsgames y la simulación lúdica. *Estudios pedagógicos, 46*(3), 123–140. https://doi.org/10.4067/S0718-07052020000300123

De Santis-Piras, A., & Morales Morante, L. (2019). Dispositivos móviles y las multiplataforma de interacción lúdica. In A. Torres Toukumidis, L. Romero-Rodríguez, & J. Salgado Guerrero (Eds.), *Juegos y Sociedad: desde la interacción a la inmersión para el cambio social* (pp. 69–78). Ciudad de México: McGraw Hill.

Donovan, T. (2010). *Replay: the history of video games*. Yellow Ant.

Gando, L. (2021). Bayes Esports: Desafíos para el sector de deportes electrónicos en 2021. *SBCNoticias*. https://sbcnoticias.com/bayes-esports-desafios-para-el-sector-de-deportes-electronicos-en-2021/

Goal. (2021). ¿Qué es eSports? Por qué son un deporte y desde cuándo existen. https://www.goal.com/es/noticias/que-es-esports-por-que-deporte-desde-cuando-existen/1ghvdp5r933vg17gbvvqaq2pbg

Haibach, P., Reid, G., & Collier, D. (2017). *Motor learning and development* (2nd ed.). Human Kinetics.

Hamari, J., & Sjöblom, M. (2017). What is esports and why do people watch it? *Internet Research, 27*(2), 211–232. https://doi.org/10.1108/intr-04-2016-0085

Hilvoorde, I. V., & Pot, N. (2016). Embodiment and fundamental motor skills in esports. *Sport, Ethics and Philosophy, 10*(1), 14–27. https://doi.org/10.1080/17511321.2016.1159246

Hou, J., Yang, X., & Panet, E. (2013). How about playing games as a career? The evolution of e-sports in the eyes of mainstream media and public relations. *International Journal of Sport Communication, 13*(1), 1–21. https://doi.org/10.1123/ijsc.2019-0060

Hutchins, B., & Rowe, D. (2012). *Sport beyond television: the internet, digital media and the rise of networked media sport*. Routledge.

Jenny, S. E., Manning, R. D., Keiper, M. C., & Olrich, T. W. (2016). Virtual(ly) athletes: where esports fit within the definition of "sport." *Quest, 69*(1), 1–18. https://doi.org/10.1080/00336297.2016.1144517

Jin, D. Y. (2010). *Korea's online gaming empire*. MIT Press.

Jonasson, K., & Thiborg, J. (2010). Electronic sport and its impact on future sport. *Sport in Society, 13*(2), 287–299. https://doi.org/10.1080/1743043090 3522996

Kardefelt-Winther, D. (2014). A conceptual and methodological critique of Internet addiction research: towards a model of compensatory Internet use. *Computers in Human Behavior, 31*, 351–354. https://doi.org/10.1016/j. chb.2013.10.059

Karhulahti, V. (2017). Reconsidering esport: economics and executive ownership. *Physical Culture and Sport. Studies and Research, 74*(1), 43–53. https://doi.org/10.1515/pcssr-2017-0010

Kelly, K. (1993, de junio de 6). The first online sports game. Netrek is mind hockey on the net. *Wired.* https://www.wired.com/1993/06/netrek/

Kent, S. L. (2001). *The ultimate history of video games*. Prima.

Li, R. (2017). *Good luck have fun: the rise of eSports*. Skyhorse.

Macey, J., Hamari, J., Sjöblom, M., & Törhönen, M. (2021, april de del 7 al 10 de). Relationships between the consumption of gamblified media and associated gambling activities in a sample of esports fans. In *5th International GamiFIN Conference 2021* (GamiFIN 2021), Finland.

Marca. (2021). League of Legends fue el eSport más visto de 2021. *Redacción eSports.* https://www.marca.com/claro-mx/esports/2022/02/02/61fabf-da268e3eb5078b45e3.html

Newzoo. (2021). Newzoo's Global Esports & Live Streaming Market Report 2021. https://newzoo.com/insights/trend-reports/newzoos-global-esports-live-streaming-market-report-2021-free-version/

Olsen, K. (2007, de mayo de 21). South Korean gamers get a sneak peek at 'StarCraft II'. *USA Today.* https://usatoday30.usatoday.com/tech/gaming/2007-05-21-starcraft2-peek_N.htm

Pires, K., & Simon, G. (2015, March). Youtube live and twitch: a tour of user-generated live streaming systems. In *Proceedings of the 6th ACM Multimedia Systems Conference* (pp. 225–230). https://doi.org/10.1145/2713168. 2713195

Polsson, K. (2012). *Chronology of arcade video games*. http://vidgame.info/arcade/index.htm

Schubert, M., Drachen, A., & Mahlmann, T. (2016). Esports analytics through encounter detection. In *Proceedings of the MIT Sloan Sports Analytics Conference* (pp. 1458–1475). Boston, MIT Sloan.

Sjöblom, M., & Hamari, J. (2017). Why do people watch others play video games? An empirical study on the motivations of Twitch users. *Computers in Human Behavior, 75*, 985–996. https://doi.org/10.1016/j.chb.2016.10.019

Taylor, T. L. (2012). *Raising the stakes: e-sports and the professionalization of computer gaming*. MIT Press.

Tejera, D. (2013, de marzo de 18). League of Legends llega a 5 millones de jugadores simultáneos. *As.com.* https://as.com/meristation/2013/03/18/noticias/1363562340_114542.html

Toffler, A. (1970). *Future shock.* Bantam Books.

Waigh, M. J. (2021, de noviembre de 21). La evolución de los deportes electrónicos. *Marca*, Esports. https://www.marca.com/esports/2021/11/21/619a47d946163f84608b45f3.html

Note

1 Wikipedia (s.f.). Electronic Entertainment Expo. https://es.wikipedia.org/wiki/Electronic_Entertainment_Expo#E3_1997.

Part II

Media Platforms and Esports

2 The Social Media Impact of Esports

The Case of Esports on Facebook

*Roberto Alejandro López Novelo, José Ángel
Garfias Frías, Daniel Barredo-Ibáñez, and
Paulo Carlos López-López*

Introduction

Electronic sports have had a wide growth in recent years, which has affected the interest of different actors to get involved in them by exploring new communication, advertising and business models for a sector. A 54% of the public is between 21 and 35 years old, a group that is increasingly difficult to reach through traditional means (SuperData, 2017, p. 16). Social networks are a widely used tool to promote them and generate communities that enjoy competitions or game sessions with professional cyber athletes.

In the present work, a study was carried out based on the content analysis of a *Facebook* page called *Esports State*, in which the interactions that exist between its users are interpreted. The main objective of this investigation is to understand how this social network works to promote electronic sports within the community itself.

The analysis categories were built from a framework developed under the concept of social capital that considers esports as part of the gamer culture. The virtue of esports lies in the fact that teams or communities are created on a daily basis, in which there is a tangible accumulation of social capital that acts for the benefit of the community or individually.

The relationship between Web 2.0 and social media

Social media can be defined as platforms that allow the syndication of ideas, writings or contents. These platforms use communication, interrelation and publication tools on the Internet in order to facilitate and encourage the participation of individuals in the network. For Ozturk and Ayvaz (2018), social media have become an essential part of people's daily routine (p. 136). The key to the interest these platforms

DOI: 10.4324/9781003273691-4

has lies in the enormity of the offer, which tends to correspond to a personalization of demand:

> The Internet is currently presented as a technology that enables communication forms and processes to be potentiated… By potentiating these modes, practices and communication processes, the Internet becomes a highly attractive technosocial development for people, since in this network there are "n" number of digital environments, tools and applications, ideal for leisure and entertainment consumption in various forms and formats.
>
> (López, 2021, p. 27)

Through social media, conversations are established between members of a community. In these media, communities replace audiences, since the latter are based on unidirectional communication from mass media and social media on bidirectional and multidirectional communication dynamics (Barredo Ibáñez, 2021).

Along these lines are the contributions of Tim O'Reilly (2007), who emphasizes that the new applications that arise from Web 2.0 facilitate the construction of collaboration networks between individuals, which allows the existence of a participative web architecture, that is to say, the potential of the Internet for communication, interaction and social relations is potentiated with the increase in users.

The evolution of the systems or services offered by the Internet has also generated a new logic to understand the potential of the Internet's digital environments. We can understand Web 2.0 as applications, utilities and Internet services that are stored on a database, which can be constantly modified by users, either in content or in the way of presenting them. Web 2.0 refers to environments, applications, technology and uses, and therein lies its complexity.

According to Cobo and Pardo (2007), Tim O'Reilly establishes the constitutive principles of Web 2.0 the world wide web as a work platform, the strengthening of collective intelligence, database management as a basic competence, the end software release cycle, lightweight programming models for simplicity, software not limited to a single device and enriched user experiences.

All these characteristics make Web 2.0 a techno-social development, through which network users can carry out endless activities for their own benefit or for the common benefit of other users, making use of new systems for communication, collaboration, participation, etc., offered by this development that is changing the way we understood its predecessor, Web 1.0, a one-way web.

Social media and Esports

A social network is a structure formed by individuals and organizations that connect to establish various types of relationships, such as a community of neighbors, a fan club, among others. Although those indicated are analogic social networks, digital ones offer the distinctive possibility of creating communities and social capital. This is possible because these sites allow the data and web applications hosted on their domain to become independent and shared by multiple users. Thus, regardless of the types of networks existing on the Internet (i.e., leisure, social relations, professionals, games), it is common for users to use these networks to establish practices of interaction, social relations and communication links with other users.

Social networks on the Internet are based on various platforms and applications, generated from Web 2.0, which enables social relations, interactivity, interaction, collaboration, communication, among network users. If the universe of these networks is observed, it will be possible to find that millions of users use the Internet daily for different purposes such as socialization, creation of communities, research, education, search for information and, in recent years, for video games and electronic devices.

Thus, social media offer a new architecture of social networks, which allows a user greater participation and collaboration, that is, they are presented as a new social space in which various processes, practices and communication dynamics are developed. At the same time, video games are a massive product that uses technological innovation and creativity in content, which together with various commercial strategies seek to recover the investment made in their development. A video game is a closed system in which various objectives or tasks must be fulfilled in an environment subject to certain rules that the player must adhere to (Salen & Zimmerman, 2004).

Electronic sports are a complementary modality to video games that generate an additional factor of interest to the industry, which in recent years has grown steadily. According to data: "In 2019, a global esports audience of 395 million was registered, including enthusiasts and casual viewers, and it is expected that by 2023 this figure will exceed 645 million people" (Statista, 2021).

Esports must be understood as video games whose structure and rules allow competition between users, thereby promoting competitive practice. In addition, when a video game reaches this category by consensus of the gaming community, companies and associations, institutionalized bodies are created. These bodies monitor compliance with the rules of the game to measure the results of the confrontations and create a competitive space where victory is determined by the ability of the participants, who train to improve in video games.

The relationship between video games and sport that has given rise to the concept of "electronic sport" has roots that can be traced to authors such as Bernard Suits (2007), who offers notions to distinguish the transition from a game to a sport, which goes from the first to the second when certain conditions are met, among them "that it be a game of skill, that the skill is physical, that the game has a wide base of followers and that these elements have a certain level of stability" (p. 14). All these conditions are fulfilled by video games in their entirety, because although it is blamed that there is no physical activity in them, the truth is that the reflexes of the hand and the eye must be trained as in any other sport.

With regard to the fan base that follows sports, it is worth noting the degree of interest that electronic sports generate through broadcasts so that the public can watch live competitions both in streaming and on television channels, including some of them dedicated specifically for this purpose, to professional gamers. In addition, we must not lose sight of the market for content and commentary programs that are made with electronic sports and video games, as is the case of the Twitch platform, which has found a niche market in these streamers to continue expanding this activity. It is noteworthy that currently the consumption of electronic sports content is so wide since there are many video games that adopt this scheme with their own leagues, public and business models, which guarantees a wide range of content. This is where social networks come into play to accompany gamers and the public in their shared experiences around electronic sports.

Gamer culture and electronic sports

A framework that will encompass the relationship between social media and electronic sports is the concept of gamer culture, which will serve as the basis for understanding what it means today to be a participant in activities linked to esports. Regarding gamer culture, the category should be divided into the two words that make it up: culture and gamer. One of the most precise definitions of culture is presented by Geertz, who says that "culture is a network of meanings" (2003) and as such is composed of symbolic elements that represent and have different meanings which must be understood in different ways. As a whole, hence the idea of a framework.

In this way, a gamer culture will have to do with what happens inside video games and the related phenomena around them. Researchers such as Franz Mäyrä (2008) have even recognized the importance of studying the video game as a cultural product and, therefore, a framework of action must be recognized that goes far beyond what happens in the experience with the game itself and expands toward what happens in the context of the player's own action with other stakeholders. For a long time, the gamer culture was somewhat criticized and full of prejudices, linking video games to issues such as violence or wasting time, but over time the concept of the word video games has been consolidated in academic fields and this has expanded their scope of action toward more positive activities, changing the conception of them (Garfias & Cervera, 2017).

The phenomenon of electronic sports cannot be understood outside of gamer culture, where live competition streaming services connect with the fan culture that has been generated around them. This phenomenon is defined as a new wave in electronic sports, which begins around 2010 and is characterized by the growth of live streaming through the combination of television with social and public interaction (Taylor, 2018). The last edition of the *League of Legends World Championship 2020*, held at the end of that year, had an average audience of 23 million viewers (Rodríguez, 2020, December 9), generating more interest in sponsorships and business models for large companies.

At a more individual level, there is the case of streamers, who begin with the creation of video content about video games, either as live streaming or as videos on demand on platforms such as *Twitch*, *Facebook* or *YouTube*, among others. These contents produced 5.2 billion dollars in revenue and reached 850 million users during 2018 as reported by SuperData (2019, p. 13). Streamer revenue comes from paid channel subscriptions, and percentages of revenue from ads on platforms, user donations and sponsorships.

In this way, it is possible to observe a lot of opportunities in activities related to electronic sports, which has activated the interest of many actors who want to participate, either personally or institutionally, in an activity that attracts the attention of large audiences in a global form.

Social capital and Esports

Esports are today presented as a complex and attractive object of study in which social capital finds a laboratory to carry out new and innovative analyses. Social capital is a concept in which elements such as social relations, social support, social cohesion, norms, values, trust, cooperation, etc., are concentrated. Pierre Bourdieu (1985) defines social capital as a potential or current aggregate of resources that accumulate in an individual or social group through the generation of lasting relationships or contacts that are more or less institutionalized and of mutual agreement and recognition (p. 248). Thus, social capital is determined by the size of the relationships and networks that the individual has built, and the use that individuals make of the existing resources in the previously established connections and networks. Bourdieu views social capital as a collective form of advantage acquired by members of a network (López, 2011, p. 65).

James Coleman (1990) defines social capital as a variety of entities that have two elements in common: all individuals are part of the social structure and, likewise, some actions of the actors that make up said social structure are facilitated. For Coleman, social capital can be anything or any situation that facilitates individual or collective action in a society, detached from social networks, reciprocity and truth. Robert Putnam (1995) establishes that the central point of social capital is the generalized principle of reciprocity and, in this sense, defines social capital as "the advantages that emerge from social organizations such as trust, norms and connections, which allow the efficiency of society by facilitating coordinated actions" (p. 167). One of the most interesting contributions of this author on the concept of social capital is the analysis of relationships of trust, the role played by social networks and regulatory systems and the way in which all this influences the degree of community cooperation. Thus, it establishes that within a community the constitution of social capital is associated with dense and horizontal social networks, which today are enhanced by the presence of information and communication technologies (ICTs).

Francis Fukuyama (1995) understands social capital as the specific existence of informal values or established norms among the members of a group that allow cooperation and the construction of trust between them; "social capital is a capacity that originates from the prevalence of confidence in society or in certain parts of it" (p. 26). From this perspective, the acquisition of social capital requires the assimilation of moral norms of the community, as well as the endowment of virtues such as loyalty, honesty and dependency. Nahapiet and Ghoshal (1988) suggest that social capital should be studied in three fundamental dimensions: structural, relational and cognitive. The structural dimension refers to the ability of individuals to establish weak and strong relationships or ties with other individuals within a system. The relational dimension focuses on the character of the connections between individuals. This dimension is best understood through trust and identification between members of a network. Thus, when trust relationships are generated within the network, the actors develop a reputation of being worthy of trust, which can become important information for the network actors. The cognitive dimension refers to the common interest or the attitude of the members of a network of wanting to share their knowledge within an organization, based on the principle of mutual trust.

From everything that has been said up to this point, it can be established that, since the Internet is a structure that has become increasingly present in the dynamics of individuals who are immersed in this new context, it can be thought that this technology has potential for the construction of new forms of social capital. In electronic sports, the fundamental elements that shape social capital are present: social relationships, support, participation, norms, values, trust, collaboration and cooperation. These elements come to life in the daily processes of the game, since they are found within the community of players or fans, and can be used in different ways. The virtue of esports lies in the fact that teams or communities are created on a daily basis, in which there is a tangible accumulation of social capital that acts for the benefit of the community or individually. Thus, social capital allows us to carry out a critical analysis of electronic sports; formally understand the importance of social relationships; analyze the social structures in which game dynamics are generated (connections between players and fan communities) and, above all, adequately dimension an interesting and complex study phenomenon due to its economic, media, cultural and social scope.

Methodology

Once we have defined the concepts of social media, social networks, electronic sports and social capital, what follows is to analyze the way in which social media serve to promote the practice, consumption and fanaticism of sports within the electronic community itself. For this purpose, a *Facebook* group with these characteristics was selected, with the aim of doing a content analysis with the categories from social capital, in order to make a correct interpretation of the content, since electronic sports as a cultural and creative product are complex networks of meanings. The starting point is to describe the *Esports State* community of *Facebook* group that served as the case study. This group functions as an intermediary between electronic sports competitions, companies seeking to advertise and the public interested in what is happening in the competitive scene. *Esports State* can be defined as a creator of institutional content around electronic sports whose main interest is to promote and boost the consumption of electronic sports in Mexico and Latin America as a result of the growth of this activity in recent years.

Esports State was consolidated as a company based on a business model built on synergies that allows them to manage talent by operating as viewers that recruit talented players to prepare and guide them in formal competitions as well as advice so that they can stream their content. Also, in the second instance, they participate in the organization of tournaments in online and offline mode so that a space is created to sponsor and offer entertainment options to the public, which is primarily young. And, in the third instance, they contribute to the development of advertising campaigns in virtual reality that serve to activate the events they organize, as mentioned on their website esportstate.com. The role of an intermediary that they assume means that they are well connected both with companies and with the community of esports fans.

In order to communicate with fans and convey its vision, *Esports State* has built a corporate identity through logos and institutional colors to distinguish itself. In this way, the *Esports State* social network communication plan seeks to generate its own identity in its publications and to captivate and attract more public to its group, they use the main social networks at their disposal such as *YouTube, Twitter, Instagram, Discord* and of course *Facebook*; it is in the latter where the analysis was carried out. At the time of the last consultation, in January 2022, the *Esports State Facebook* page had 143,588 followers, the content publication rate was at least three daily contents, which included memes, interviews, videos with news, infographics or live broadcasts of tournaments which are commented on by the community. Within *Facebook* they are defined as a group that creates video game content and videos that serves so that the community can enjoy exclusive tournaments and events, meet other gamers, while offering sponsored content, which circulates in the other social networks that they manage but adapted for this end.

It would have to be said then that this community has behind it an interest that pursues commercial ends but that the community receives it for the usefulness it finds in its contents to formalize the construction of a gamer community contrasted with the others for its unique identity. What is sought is to answer the following research questions: What role do social networks play in the esports community? What level of interaction exists between community managers and users? What content do esports enthusiasts share? The objective is to trace a clear and systematized path in social networks toward esports, since "when people with a shared interest can come together in a multiplayer game, there is the possibility of a positive and prosocial interaction between them, both within as out of the game" (Molyneux et al., 2015, p. 2). In this idea are present the fundamental elements for a content analysis based on the categories of social capital.

The methodology used is content analysis to evaluate the role played by social networks in the interaction with esports, that is, to understand the social capital generated by social media, using the analysis dimensions proposed by Nahapiet and Goshal (1988), particularly the cognitive dimension that refers to the common interest or the attitude of the members of a network of wanting to share their knowledge within an organization, based on the principle of mutual trust. Likewise, this dimension refers to the resources that are latent in each of the members of a structure, organization or network. This dimension also refers to the existence of a mutual understanding between the members of a network. This understanding is achieved through the use of a common language and the willingness of individuals to exchange not only their knowledge and information, but also their experiences.

For Klaus Krippendorff (1990) content analysis is a research technique aimed at formulating, based on certain data, reproducible and valid inferences that can be applied to their context. Thus, content analysis includes special processes and procedures to treat scientific data, and its purpose is to provide knowledge. It is necessary to mention that this technique basically studies communication or messages, within the framework of the relationships established between the sender and the receiver. Thus, content analysis allows us to study what is being said, that is, it is the study of the characteristics of the content of the message; and to define what is the central theme and the subthemes that are immersed in a message or content.

The content analysis is based on a study of the publications made by *Esports State* in a 30-day period that was from December 27, 2021, to January 27, 2022. In the first observation, a count was made of the most recurrent types of publications on the platform, where there are four main contents that feed it: live broadcasts, videos with news, news images and memes. In this sense, the comments on the live broadcasts were analyzed to categorize them according to the following variables:

- *Common interest*: that what is discussed is actually about electronic sports and not about other topics, reinforcing bringing the discussion to the topic of esports.
- *Confidence in the organization*: what users talk about in relation to the video game brand, companies or even the *Esports State*.

- *Mutual understanding*: that terms or concepts of the gamer culture community be used, that is, other games or characters that have appeared in different sagas.
- *Exchange of knowledge and experiences*: telling an anecdote or comment to help the community or giving references to other sites.

Results

From the selected sample of the *Esports State Facebook* page, the content strategy used was to identify, periodically posting between two and three daily publications distinguished under the following categories:

- *Streaming*: live broadcasts of professional players with an average duration of two hours where they showed their skills and gave players tips to compete online. Or, they were constituted as a space for dialogue in the case of non-competition video games to demonstrate skills. The most frequently played video games were *Halo Infinity* and *Call of Duty Mobile* positioned as competitive video games. However, gameplays of *The Legend of Zelda Skyward Sword HD, Metroid Dread* and *God of War for PC* were also shown. All these games went on sale last year and are valid within the gamer community.
- *News videos*: where they used John "Nosurname" as an influencer to publicize relevant events of recent months.
- *News images*: where they are always accompanied by the institutional colors in purple and black of the company with a headline and deepen the comment.
- *Memes*: Comic images in relation to daily events within the gamer culture accompanied most of the time with a background with the institutional colors of the *Esports State* company.

In this way the following data was obtained:

Table 2.1 Type of contents on the *Facebook* account of *Esports State*

Type of content	Posts	Reactions	Comments	Shared
Streaming	19	398	3,125	217
News videos	3	402	11	126
Image with news	18	12,476	211	117
Memes	10	7,793	195	717
Total	50	21,069	3,542	1,177

From the review of these data, it is observed that the main contents are streaming and images with news, with streaming being the main content of the page with 3,125 comments, which indicates that the exchange of information between the members of this network is constant and is based on the principle of collaboration and trust between users. In the case of images with news, Table 2.1 tells us that the highest number of reactions – 12,476 – is obtained in this category, which allows us to infer that the users of this network not only publish textual comments, but also express their interest in the contents of the page through other forms of action. On the other hand, memes are the content that is shared the most with 717 units; this is due in the first instance to its viral quality and, finally, news videos, being published less frequently, are not essential content for the site.

These data clearly show that social media are currently presented as socio-technical spaces through which users who like esports establish diverse and different forms of not only communication (enhanced by the characteristics of these media), but also elements such as participation, collaboration, trust that emerge from the theory of social capital used in this work. Now, since streaming is the content that generated the most comments, a content analysis was carried out where the comments were categorized in relation to the variables described above, which try to analyze the social capital that is generated in the followers of streaming on this space. The following results were obtained:

The construction of Table 2.2 is derived from the analysis of the comments generated throughout 19 live broadcasts that were identified in this period according to the proposed categories. In the case of common interest, it was possible to see that a large part of the discussion within live streaming is around the issue of esports; reinforcing the interest of fans in the content made by streamers, this trend reiterates that what is said effectively revolves around electronic sports and does not talk about other topics.

Table 2.2 Type of comments shared on live streamings on the *Facebook* account of *Esports State*

Type of comment	Quantity
Common interest	424
Trust on the organization	73
Mutual understanding	310
Knowledge exchange	123
Others	1,597
Total	2,562

Regarding trust in the organization (that users talk in relation to the video game brand, companies or even *Esports State*), it was found that they are not so concerned about the link with the organizations that generate the content of the page of *Facebook* or a critique of video game companies, for these members of the network, the practices, dynamics and strategies of the game per se are more important than any other notion. In the case of mutual understanding (the use of terms or concepts specific to the gamer culture community, that is, other games or characters that have appeared in different sagas), non-significant data was found, since there are very few specialized comments around video games. Finally, when it comes to knowledge sharing, the data shows that very few network members actually share meaningful and important information, and allow the streamer to be the one in charge of this process. Based on the above, we can observe that the principles that emanate from the theory of social capital, both traditional and on the Internet, are present in social media, in this particular case, on the *Esports State* page, although not exponentially.

Conclusions

The management of social networks by any project that is currently undertaken is important, given the existing link between these media and everyday life (López, 2021; Ozturk & Ayvaz, 2018). In the case of electronic sports, it becomes much more important due to the large number of young users who are interested in the subject; if anything, the point to improve is to find better ways to create content and obtain results. In the case of live streaming, it is found that this has become very important for electronic sports and for this reason spaces such as *Facebook* have created the *Facebook Gaming* division to promote it within their spaces and compete against other social networks such as *Twitch* that have done from the beginning.

It is necessary to delve deeper into what makes it attractive to watch others play, because, beyond competencies, social media serve as a space for sociability processes within the community itself, similar to the approaches made by the authors cited in this text regarding social capital. These game spaces' broadcast on social networks allow us to observe that a large part of the streaming comments is presented within a defined group that has common objectives with respect to esports. Regarding memes, it is established that, due to their viral nature, they are part of the gamer culture, promoting their dissemination in the community. In this study, it was found that, through them, they seek to obtain income from advertising and sponsorship.

To conclude these reflections, it is important to point out that, regardless of the platform, interaction through online social networks fosters dynamics and processes of social relationships, interaction and trust, to mention a few variables of social capital. Thus, it is clear that digital social media focused on topics related to esports contribute to a greater or lesser extent to the creation of social capital in its traditional and online form.

References

Barredo Ibáñez, D. (2021). *Medios digitales, participación y opinión pública.* Tirant Lo Blanch.

Bourdieu, P. (1985). The forms of capital. In J. G. Richardson (Ed.), *Handbook for theory and research for the sociology of education* (pp. 15–29). Greenwood.

Cobo, C., & Kuklinsky, H. (2007) *Planeta web 2.0. Inteligencia Colectiva o medios Fast Food.* FLACSO.

Coleman, J. (1990) *Foundations of social theory.* Belknap.

Fukuyama, F. (1995) *Trust: the social virtues and the creation of prosperity.* The Free Press.

Garfias, J., & Cervera, A. (2017). *Cambios en la concepción de los videojuegos. En Molina y Vedia, Silvia. Sentido y formas del cambio.* UNAM.

Geertz, C. (2003). *La interpretación de las culturas.* Gedisa.

Krippendorff, K. (1990). *Metodología del análisis de contenido. Teoría y Práctica.* Paidós.

López, R. (2011). *La construcción del capital social en las redes sociales en Internet: Discutamos México en Facebook* [Ph.D. Thesis]. Universidad Autónoma de México.

López, R. (2021). *Ocio y entretenimiento en el contexto digital. Aproximaciones desde la academia.* GEDISA.

Mäyrä, F. (2008). *An introduction to game studies. Games in culture.* Sage.

Molyneux, M., Vasudevan, K., & Zuñiga, H. (2015). Gaming social capital: exploring civic value in multiplayer videogames. *Journal of Computer Mediated Communication, 20*(4), 381–399.

Nahapiet, J., & Ghosal, S. (1998) Social capital, intellectual capital, and the organizational advantage. *Academy of Management Review, 23*(2), 242–266.

O'Reilly, T. (2007). What is web 2.0: design patterns and business models for the next generation of software. *Communications & Strategies*, No. 1, First Quarter.

Ozturk, N., & Ayvaz, S. (2017) Sentiment analysis on Twitter: a text mining approach to the Syrian refugee crisis. *Telematics and Informatics, 35*(1), pp. 136–147.

Putnam, R. (1995). Bowling alone. America's declining social capital. *Journal of Democracy, 6*, 65–78.

Rodríguez, D. (2020, December 9). *League of legends bate records de audiencia en las finales de Worlds 2020. 23 millones de espectadores.* https://www. hobbyconsolas.com/noticias/league-legends-bate-records-audiencia-finales-worlds-2020-23-millones-espectadores-770929

Salen, K., & Zimmerman, E. (2004). *Rules of play. Game design fundamentals.* The MIT Press.

Statista. (2021). *Evolución anual de espectadores de las competencias de videojuegos a nivel mundial entre 2015 y 2023.* https://es.statista.com/estadisticas/711557/audiencia-anual-de-esports-a-nivel-mundial/

Suits, B. (2007). The elements of sport. In W. J. Morgan (Ed.), *Ethics in sport* (2nd ed., pp. 9–20). Human Kinetics.

SuperData. (2017). *Esports courtside: playmakers of 2017.* https://www.super-dataresearch.com/market-data/esports-market-report/

SuperData. (2019). *2018 year in review. Digital games and interactive media.* https://www.superdataresearch.com

Taylor, T. L. (2018). *Watch me play: Twitch and the rise of game live streaming.* Princeton University Press.

Part III

Communicative Globalization of Esports

3 Live-Streaming Culture in the Esports Community

Javier F. A. Vega Ramírez and
Erika Lucía González Carrión

A Definition of Esports

To define Esports, we need to take a look at their origins, which date back to the official video game competitions. The first of these was held at Stanford University on October 19, 1972, and involved the video game Spacewar! created by Steve Russell in 1962. At this event, Stanford students were invited to the Intergalactic Spacewar Olympics, and the first prize was a year's subscription to Rolling Stone. Bruce Baumgart won the five-man free-for-all individual event, and Slim Tovar and Robert E. Maas won the team competition.

The first documented large-scale championship was organized by Atari in 1980, starring the video game Space Invaders, developed by Tomohiro Nishikado and manufactured and sold by Taito Co in 1978. With a much greater focus on advertising (which set it apart from the Standford Spacewar tournament, whose intention was more focused on scientific achievement), it attracted 10,000 participants from across the United States, establishing video game competitions from that moment forth, which continue to be a common activity until the present day. Although in this sense we still cannot talk about full-fledged Esports (as we will discuss further on), these events represent two fundamental milestones that illustrate the importance of the regulated game due to large-scale participation.

In the 1990s, the explosive growth of the internet and the popularization of the World Wide Web resulted in the mass production of games for personal computers. These were the early days of games that were not dependent on a specific console (as is the case with Nintendo) and a growth in popularity of player interconnectivity through servers. One of the pioneers in this architectural network design was the game Netrek created by Smith & Silvey in 1988. It had a gameplay for 16 simultaneous players and was the first game to use metaservers and

DOI: 10.4324/9781003273691-6

the first to store information on frequent users. These elements led it to be credited by *Wired* magazine as "the first online sports game" in 1993 (Kelly, 1993).

This brought on the age of the grand tournaments, highlighting the Nintendo World Championships in 1990, touring several parts of the United States, and the world finals were held at Universal Studios Hollywood in California. Nintendo held a second world championship in 1994 called Nintendo PowerFest '94, where 132 people made it to the finals in San Diego, California, and Mike Iarossi finally took first place. Blockbuster Video also had its own world video game championship in the early 1990s, co-organized by the magazine *GamePro*. It brought in competitors from the United States, Canada, the United Kingdom, Australia and Chile. The 1994 video game championships included games such as NBA Jam and Virtual Racing.

According to Márquez (2017), the unemployment crisis that hit South Korea in the early 1990s, coupled with the rise of the internet and growth of cybercafés, resulted in a large number of people available to play video games. The Korean Ministry of Culture took advantage of this boom and built on it, creating the Korea e-Sports Association (KeSPA), which in turn led to a television niche in the transmission and retransmission of the StarCraft and Warcraft III championships on open television 24 hours a day. This history provides the backdrop for a discussion on the elements that distinguish video games from Esports.

Conceptualizing games, play, sports and Esports

Games and play

For a proper conceptualization, we must address the terminology associated with games, play, video games and Esports to fully comprehend how a once recreational activity began to take on a competitive and eventually athletic quality from a global perspective. An initial approach is to look at the fundamental differentiation between sport and game, where both are understood to be recreational activities that fictionalize a dimension of reality, coordinating its common space in pursuit of interaction.

Therefore, when we look at the epistemology of the game, we find the following definitions:

- From an 18th-century perspective, it was a recreational way to pass leisure time (Scheuerl, 1994).

- From a more 19th-century perspective, it was a way to exercise strength and virtue, under the conceptualization that it prepares you for daily life and is associated with to entertainment.
- And from a more 20th-century approach, we can discuss the game as a cathartic process that stimulates the spirit over other superficial strengths or energies, closer to psychoanalysis (Toro, 2021).

As Toro (2021) observes, according to Pellegrini (2011), the differentiation between "game" and "play" as conceptualizations of the term "juego" in Spanish addresses the different meaning behind the action in terms of involvement. Whereas the word "jugar" in Spanish is a multiple action that can serve to recreate a world or compete within a set of rules (in this context, playing ring around the roses has the same level of involvement as playing a soccer game), the word "play" in English requires the immersion into a process that, even when full of rules, is an interpretation of the world and therefore its fiction responds to the structure of a regulated sport, with physical action and a respect for structures, unlike the "game", which refers to a specific objectual structure without the structural and transcendental derivations of "play".

This differentiation can help us to comprehend the connection between sport and game, depending on the baseline epistemology that the notion of "juego" responds to. "Juego" under the conceptualization of "to play" responds to a logic of active development of all human functions, in representation of a broad interaction with the environment. It is the closest to sport that we can observe in its classic vision, whereas the conceptualization of "to game" refers to the specific objectual recreation, more closely related to recreational use, and adds the complexity that its recreation of the real world is more limited by self-contained rules.

This also makes the passage from game to sport determinant in the relationship between traditional sport and Esport, considering that each stance perceived is connected based on the original meaning and use detected, provoking discordance phenomena between similar dialoguing contexts, like what occurs between the International Olympic Committee (IOC) and the Olympic Council of Asia (OCA), who do not hold the same conceptualization in practice of what is considered Esport and what is not considered sport.

Sports and Esports

To address the issue of what can and cannot be considered Esports, we must first make a differentiation between activity and sport (Rodríguez et al., 2009). According to most research, sport is considered to be a fun or competitive activity that has the following characteristics:

a   A well-known and established set of rules (that are not agreed upon at each stage, nor are they arbitrarily defined).
b   A community of practice (widespread in the sense that it is not a game closed only to the creators, as is the case with certain board games).
c   Physical activity taken to a level of specialization (that exceeds the threshold of simple natural movement, where its execution is intentional).

For this reason, the debate on the table is whether the practice of video games can enter into the category of Esports. Issues include:

a   Regarding the "well-known set of rules": A lack of stability in the rules, which can be modified from one update to another (although never radically), means that there is a difference between video games. The virtualization of a sport (such as the experience of the IOC in the 2020 Olympic Games), which contemplates rules that are relatively similar to the physical sport, is not the same as the development of a video game played by different players in seasons, versions or qualifiers (such as Fortnite).
b   Regarding the "community of practice": This element is applicable to any sporting activity that has a development in itself. In this sense, the community of practice is differentiated based on the purpose applied to each activity. For example, FGC does not give a competitive purpose like the Olympic sport does to its associativity. On the other hand, associativity with the intention of winning tournaments responds to the structure of traditional sports clubs, even including supragroup regulations that serve as a factor of cohesion and control.

On this level, the role developed by transmission channels is particularly important, in terms of both streaming channels and broadcasting channels.

–   The main streaming channel (which can be named for its sense of community) is Twitch (twitch.tv), whose access and transmission is monetizable, although its use is unlimited. TwitchTracker (TwitchTracker.com), the site for consult Twitch statistics, indicates that in the first week of February (2022), 2,932.583 viewers logged on, reaching an all-time online viewing record of 6,577,002 viewers.

- The other channel that generates a sense of community is Discord (discord.com), which is a service that provides rooms for voice transmission (VoIP voice chat, video and text chat). It is used for smaller transmissions, although it has a high calling in a non-widespread community sense.
- There are several broadcasting channels, depending on the country and the purpose. They often work as stabilized vicarious events (in Chile, the ETC channel). Widespread transmission has its limitations depending on the type of access device (a phenomenon under review).
- Physical activity taken to a level of specialization. This element is complex. Although we can successfully establish a difference between the player who plays using their intellectual prowess but from a seated position (such as in chess) and the player who shows their dexterity through other competencies, once again from a seated position, the effective physical exertion of the player can be equivalent to ongoing exercise in each round (Jiménez & Araya, 2012). In children we consider the practice of "active" video games (exergaming) as intense exercise (Pérez, 2019), although there are references that indicate that this is not a situation that is unique to exergames (by assuming that it is the obvious physical activity that promotes physical exertion), but rather by determined stages of the game, as can be seen through measurements taken in games like Shooter in critical stages, or when entering Call of Duty: Warzone or in competitive stages of games like FIFA (last minute) or others (Trotter et al., 2020).

This is important to highlight, because it generates consensus on the consideration of what is "sport" as opposed to the consideration of a set of rules (which would be the weakest part of the set).

- In this sense, gaming platforms strengthen this consideration with their technological development. Although the main gameplay is obtained from the personal computer (in the Steam platform), the advancing technology in Nintendo, Wii or Xbox has a direct influence.
- In the case of Nintendo, the mobility accessories (peripherals as a complement to the gaming experience) favor this, although they are generated on a case-by-case basis. For Wii, the motion-sensing device points to the sporting and gameplay experience. The most

striking case is Kinect (Xbox 360). With its high level of technology (3D body scanner for simulated imaging), it was abandoned as an accessory in 2018 and in 2020 it came back with its integration with Azure (AI), although in external applications. The most successful case study of this use is Ocuvera (Brown Kramer et al., 2020).

The estimation of sport in the sense that it represents physical exertion contemplates games with or without manual devices, although essentially games categorized as Esports are for personal computers (and therefore keyboard gameplay or adaptations, such as Surface). This element helps to establish a differentiation between the video game and Esports, based on the characteristics of the game and not on the classification of gamers, an element that depends on the profile, following Bartle's (2003) traditional player taxonomy, even though studies such as Newzoo (Bosman, 2019) make it possible to profile at least two types of gamers who participate in Esports: Ultimate Gamer and All-Round Enthusiast.

Quality of Esports

There is also a difference between a video game that is elevated to the category of Esports (through international recognition) and video games that are created as an emulation of a real sport, and whose emulation is what makes it considered a sport (and therefore an Esport).

This difference explains why a video game such as Zwift has been recognized as both a video game and an Esport (when in reality it is a virtualization environment of the cycling emulator experience) for the purposes of the Olympic Games Beijing, based on the COI guidelines, and why Street Fighter V didn't enter into the same category even though its gameplay had been announced, complete with medal events, for the Hangzhou Asian Games (2022). In fact, between the Olympic Games Beijing (2020/2021) and Hangzhou Asian Games (2022), a clear difference was established between the games chosen and their level of development (Table 3.1).

All the games accepted in exhibition mode during the Olympic Games are emulations of Olympic Games played in real competition; therefore, their consideration as sport stems from their condition as emulation, with the limitations of virtualization of the physical experience. On the other hand, the games accepted (after one presentation in exhibition mode during the Indonesia Asian Games in 2018) in the Hangzhou Asian Games (2022) will be in competition mode, with full medal events. The consideration of Esports as sports stems from

Table 3.1 Different video games according their consideration of games

Olympic Games Beijing (2020/2021)	Hangzhou Asian Games (2022)
Grand Tour, Digital Polyphony (motoring)	Honor of Kings/Arena of Valor Asian Games version
Zwift Inc. (cycling)	Dota 2
eBaseball Powerful Pro Baseball 2020 (baseball and softball)	Peacekeeper Elite/PUBG Mobile Asian Games Version
Virtual Regatta SAS (sailing and regatta)	EA Sports FIFA branded soccer games
Open Format (rowing)	Hearthstone
	League of Legends
	Dream Three Kingdoms 2
	Street Fighter V
	AESF Robot Masters (exhibition mode)
	AESF VR Sports (exhibition mode)

the analysis of the three aforementioned factors, including physical exertion, although explicitly adding adaptation to the ethical criteria and sportsmanship values respected by the OCA.

On this level, the Asian Electronic Sports Federation (AESF)s definition of Esport adequately encompasses these elements analyzed. Its official website explains:

> Literally, the word "esports" is the combination of Electronic and Sports which means using electronic devices as a platform for competitive activities. It is facilitated by electronic systems, unmanned vehicle, unmanned aerial vehicle, robot, simulation, VR, AR and any other electronic platform or object in which input and output shall be mediated by human or human-computer interfaces.
>
> (AESF, 2022)

Live-Streaming culture in the Esports community

Live streaming and broadcasting

When discussing transmission platforms, two concepts currently coexist, although their timing varies: broadcasting and live streaming. The term broadcasting is used to refer to the possibility of mass dissemination of information, implying a "profound change in mass culture", primarily by generating the opportunity for any person to "transmit in a way that is simple, cheap and accessible" (author's translation, Varona,

2018, p. 2). This aims to democratize content transmission processes, where the starting point is an emission element that simultaneously distributes information to several receptors. One of the closest examples is the work methodology of the media, whose emission is sent out from a hub to several users, who consume the content. On a widespread level, this is what television transmission makes possible in the format of open television, although the digitalization process of this resource has progressed over the years and has had a direct impact on the consumption habits of the end consumers. The main characteristic of broadcasting is providing consumers with a supply of previously generated programs whose continuity depends directly on the acceptance of these.

On the other hand, when referring to live streaming, we are talking about a "term used to refer to online means of transmission, whether these are recorded or transmitted in real time" (author's translation, Antolín et al., 2021, p. 29). There are currently several devices and media that make this transmission possible, like mobile phones or digital cameras. Over the years, live streaming has gained ground, thanks to the emergence of different platforms such as social media and others that make them possible, as well as the time dedicated by users to navigate these sites and the need for organizations, institutions and even individuals to incorporate strategies that provide visibility, and when developing a live event, users expand their options for interaction. "Live streaming platforms have become critical marketing tools and spaces that help brands to connect to their audience" (author's translation, Antolín et al., 2021, p. 30), especially those audiences that have grown up with social media.

Live-streaming possibilities are not limited to a specific sector but rather have been able to diversify in different areas, and have shown significant advantages in content production and consumption, which according to Marín (2021) include:

> Greater user proximity is possible, as well as greater immediacy and even content coverage; likewise, thanks to their accessibility it is possible to connect with audiences from their telephones or computers, at any time or place, and in real time; in terms of news, content is obtained directly from the scene, and finally, citizens play a more leading role, where they are not just consuming, but can also produce and disseminate content.
>
> (p. 57)

Based on these precisions and as a side note to this section, we incorporate criteria on the incursion of live streaming in the sports community, which in the first instance, according to González (2021), represents a true transformation in the dissemination of this type of event, where at one time television held the advantage. Furthermore, this particular environment has occupied "a prominent place in different cultures, with increasingly more people enjoying playing, watching and discussing a variety of sports" (author's translation, p. 41).

From this perspective, the sports sector, primarily those dedicated to the dissemination of these, is called upon for continual updates and incorporation of strategies and tools that allow them to respond to new forms of user consumption, and even to highlight content production by amateurs, whose accessibility to devices and the internet allows them to develop and disseminate their own products. In this sense, González (2021) says that "official coverage of sporting events by the media is evolving all the time and the media finds innovative ways to use technology to offer new angles and perspectives" (author's translation, p. 43), making it possible to highlight user content, given that high-definition images that have been produced and edited, sometimes even live, do not have the same effect as something filmed straight from a mobile phone, as well as limitations such as access to permanent connectivity.

This spectrum of consumption options, beyond sports, carries with it the exploration of new options, and, in observance of the digital surge environment, "the competitive vein of video games, which is gaining ground and is positioned through professionalization, resulting in electronic sports or Esports" (author's translation, Antón & García, 2014, p. 100). As a result of this, as indicated by Antón and García (2014), several companies are looking to "position their brand in a developing market in Spain and South America" and have already consolidated in other regions of the world like "the USA and South Korea" (author's translation, p. 100).

The role of live streaming in this context is provided by the existing multimedia convergence, where this type of transmission enters as an innovative alternative "that experiments with options from a communication standpoint and explores second screens", and out of this a new publicity market niche develops, where companies want to participate, achieve visibility and a leading role and join "the technological corporations that are already present" (author's translation, Antón & García, 2014, p. 100).

In addition to this, other authors such as Romo (2017) state that Esports emerge as "a new form of entertainment, based on a revolutionary conception of the term sport, which permeates the new generations and changes the way that media is consumed" (author's translation, p. 2), considering that these are largely consumed through digital streaming platforms, making live transmission, retransmission and interaction possible, where users play an active role in the event.

The data even asserts that this sector has been growing on a global scale and "since 2016 it has grown by 19% year after year, attracting more fans, reaching over 380 million people" (author's translation, Caro, 2021, p. 11). This has generated significant gains for the electronic gaming industry, not to mention the contribution of brands, which as previously mentioned are looking to increase visibility in this type of event, primarily in the transmission mode, making it possible to hit high numbers of views and interactions.

In this scenario that connects live streaming with Esports, one platform stands above the rest in terms of user consumption. The Twitch platform enables "real time transmissions and congregates the greatest number of simultaneous spectators" (author's translation, Carrillo, 2016, p. 3). Thanks to this type of system, the electronic gaming industry has gained ground, and from a communicational standpoint it is a clear example of the role of technology in the massification of an innovative and pluralist experience. Behind this is the opportunity for companies and organizations to develop their advertising strategies to respond to new forms of consumption.

Finally, to ratify this last point, Rodríguez (2017) indicates that Esports "due to their growth on both an economic and social level, have become a very attractive communication and information showcase". Methods such as live streaming make it possible to delve deeper into new options and the improvement "of the information ecosystem, even creating new specializations and reinventing new forms of communicating" (author's translation, p. 19), in addition to responding to new audiences.

Results of the influence of live streaming on broadcasting

As we can see, the possibilities of live-streaming Esports can directly influence broadcasting, not merely in terms of programming but as a way to influence content generation. This element, which could be considered an intuition, was examined through exploratory research developed between 2021 and 2022 in eight countries.

Instrument used

To take a deeper look into this issue, an instrument was developed to "analyze the influence of Esports transmissions in open television on online transmissions". The instrument was built based on 27 questions divided into four sections with Likert-type responses. The instrument was named "Live streaming culture in the Esports community" and underwent an adjustment and expert validation phase (six academic experts from the communications area or Esport players) and a pilot application phase for its statistical validation, and the alpha of Cronbach yielded 0.92 in 27 corrected items. The survey was applied to 206 gamers from 8 Spanish-speaking countries, and the requirement was that they were frequent video gamers. It was applied online on the Survio platform (www.survio.es) and its results were analyzed with PSPP software (GNU/Free Software Foundation, Inc., 2013). The overall results identify dissimilar profiles, with ages distributed between 12 and over 40 years old, different genders, but predominantly male, and with a variable exposure time to video games, ranging from 30 minutes to 4 hours. Likewise, the gaming device is variable (Play Station in versions 2, 3, 4 and 5, Nintendo Switch, other consoles, mobile phones and personal computers).

To analyze the results, three forms of consideration held by gamers were established previously in relation to their comprehension and conceptualization of Esports. These three forms of considering Esports were later linked to the results of the survey, to enable a comprehension of the influence between live streaming and broadcasting. The first form of consideration of Esports corresponds to gamers who feel that all video games can be considered sports. This consideration is based on the recreational profile of the sport, a profile aligned with video games and directly associated with OCA criteria and also with the classic relationship mentioned in the first section on the difference between game and sport. Once a game is established in a sense of competition, community and rules, it can be considered a sport (Rodríguez et al., 2009), an evolution that all video games can develop. A second form of comprehension of Esports is constituted by gamers who assume that only video games based on conventional sports can be considered Esports. This consideration relates to the criteria used by the IOC for the selection of Esports participants in exhibition mode during the Olympic Games Beijing (2020/2021), where the virtualization of sports through emulators or reproduction devices of the physical experience is what ends up becoming the relevant factor.

A third consideration is related to physical exertion, directly stipulating that only video games that produce physical exertion can be considered Esports. This criterion is what establishes a difference of opinion on chess or bridge (which for some specialists are sports, whereas for others they are games) although it is precisely a complex criterion to stabilize. As established by Pérez (2019),

Gutiérrez-Serafín (2019) and others, all exergame-type video games can generate physical exertion, but non-exergame video games can also generate this during a tournament (Trotter et al., 2020).

In the group surveyed, the first consideration, the assertion that all video games are sports, is the most supported (51% of positive assertions), followed by the second (35%) and finally the third consideration (32%). The fact that this criterion has the most support and is used by the OCA for the selection of video games for the Hangzhou Asian Games (2022) leads us to consider this form of comprehending Esports as a dependent variable for the relationship between live streaming and broadcasting. Likewise, it explains why associated assertions have medium to medium-high positive support, such as assertion 18. "Esport gamers are athletes" (52%), or 21. "Esports should be recognized as sports by society as a whole" (62%).

The survey established four separate sections. The first section (questions 8–15) aims to establish support for each of the three types of consideration of Esports among those surveyed. The second section (questions 16 to 21) explores the knowledge acquired about Esports based on the experience of contact with them. The third section (questions 22 to 28) explores the phenomenon of live streaming in Esports and the fourth section (questions 29 to 34) analyzes the broadcasting phenomenon in relation to Esports. Each section has distractor questions (not directly related to the intention of the topic). The object of statistical analysis of this research will therefore focus on Sections 1, 3 and 4, leaving Section 2 for future research.

Results

Upon reviewing the results, we generally see that the consideration of Esports transmission through broadcasting channels is not positive. By establishing a lineal correlation model between the assertions of the first consideration and the assertions of live streaming, the positive factor is greater (0.50) than the correlation between the same assertions and those related to broadcasting (0.47). In the review of questions of greater significance (questions 27 and 31), one from each of the groups of assertions, we can see that the correlation between both is strong (0.367). In consequence, those surveyed do not consider it positive that there is a platform transfer from live streaming to broadcasting, irrespective of the positive consideration of the transmission of Esports finals on open or paid television (given the 56% acceptance of the assertion "Esports transmission should take place on open television").

The acceptance of Esports transmission on open television speaks more of an acceptance of opportunity than a preference for television transmission. In fact, in the review of assertions on the viewing platform, the assertion "Esports finals should only be transmitted on paid channels" has an absolute rejection level of 53%, which climbs to 69% if we add those who are "almost completely in disagreement". On the other hand, the assertion "All Esports finals should be transmitted through free streaming" has 76% acceptance. Likewise, the distribution of results for the assertion "The transmission of video games on television reduces the live to just another program" does not demonstrate a preeminence of a positive or negative assertion, reaching a maximum value of 30% for "this doesn't represent me". The neutrality of this assertion can be explained by the aforementioned factor of a sense of opportunity for viewing rather than a preference over live transmission, which is confirmed when analyzing the similar distribution between the assertion "Esports transmissions should take place on open television", with an equally equitable distribution (27% for the value "this doesn't represent me").

We can see that the results obtained from the responses of participating gamers do not identify a positive outlook on broadcasting as an adoption channel for Esports transmissions, but they maintain a neutral attitude regarding the opportunity. As with live streaming, the sense of opportunity only prevails because of the relevant factor of cost. If we look at the age distribution of participants (which can give us a notion of the economic capacity of participants), we can see that the age distribution is also homogeneous (25% are people between 19 and 21, while 29% are between 26 and 30 and 12% are over 30). Therefore, economic capacity alone is not the preeminent value, but rather availability, which is coherent with the greater preference for the live-streaming channel, directly referring to free channels through Facebook (12%), YouTube (20%) and Twitch (37%).

Even though the analysis identifies some broadcasting levels that have a presence regarding Esports viewing options, with general mentions of open TV (in gamers in Ecuador and Bolivia) or specific channels, like ETC (Chile), live-streaming channels like Twitch or Discord have the greatest advantage.

We can see that live-streaming channels have a preeminence for the gaming community, because they offer unique elements (ample time, contents created around affinity, skill of players exhibited, possibility of replays on demand, low cost of viewing and production). These elements cannot be fully reproduced through television, except the low cost of viewing, which still doesn't operate with the same motives as the live-streaming channels: Open television is available through a sense of public service attributed to radio frequency. Streaming is dependent on the availability of internet, availability which is a given, since most gamers are online. Considering that the characteristics of broadcasting cannot compare to these benefits of streaming channels, the possibilities of comparison between the two are low, even though some conditions can be reproduced in digital television (such as availability of replays), but only by opening accounts on free channels (like YouTube and others).

Conclusions

The review of Esports developed throughout this chapter and the existing interrelation between live streaming and broadcasting provides an analysis of the phenomenon of video games from a broad perspective. This also helps us to comprehend why, when faced with the same elements and the same definitions, the comprehension varies from one context to the next. If we take the definition of Esports from a comprehension of game and sport, and not as physical activity and recreational activity as preeminent possibilities of collective relationship, we can understand why any video game can be considered Esport if the support for it follows the same conditions as a sport (community, rules and specialization in its execution). If we take the definition related to physical exertion, this definition is limited to electronic versions of traditional sports adapted through a specific device or video game that require movement for their execution, such as the versions of video games that require distance recognition and communication devices.

Whatever the definition of Esports adopted, the consequences can be seen in the different sporting contexts, notably both international and local Olympic Committees. This is more notable when we analyze the swift evolution and integration these have had in different athletic organizations, notably the OCA. This council has assumed the notion of Esports within the three aforementioned definitions, with the flexibility that the set of rules is established for the duration of execution or competition, irrespective of whether these may be revised after the next competition.

Even with this element in mind, the discussions around the interrelation that we can establish between live streaming and broadcasting are directly related to the way we understand the gamer culture. The notion of entertainment in relation to video games does not disappear as a result of the logic of competition for limited periods of time revolving around gamers. This is essential because the availability of spaces to share both practices and competitions is not necessarily grounded exclusively in the need for specialization among those observing other competitors, but rather in the desire to be entertained and have fun. The explosion of the World Wide Web makes it possible to share content around the world, generated by digital media and easily disseminated with minimal support. The stabilization of these dissemination media (specialized channels) does not suppress the ease of access or low cost of production. The availability of games and dissemination channels on the same platform (internet) resolves the issue of access to these for the gamer community without the need to look for other spaces, the same phenomenon that influences the transmission of Esports, irrespective of the definition adopted for these.

As a result, even when traditional media (broadcasting) seek to learn, adapt and imitate the means of interaction and communication established in the gamer community in its transmission spaces, the gamer community itself does not require traditional channels to make Esport events and competitions available. The research presented here confirms this data: The availability of Esports on open television would be highly valued. However, this is not directly required because the transmission channels themselves are sufficient to meet the community's requirements.

Finally, in light of all aspects explored above, we can assert that because the practice of Esports is a recognizable sport, albeit still lacking a general consensus around its definition, its dissemination channels are unique and easily accessible, with ongoing content generation and renovation of these at a unique speed and scale that meets the needs of gamers. Distribution channels for traditional contents, such as broadcasting, can interact around the novelty of contents produced around Esports, including the possibility to adopt these to expand their notion of supply. However, even though their availability may be positively valued, this is neither a required nor an expected space for their dissemination.

References

Asian Electronic Sports Federation [AESF] (2022). What is Esports?. *AESF's Homepage*. https://www.aesf.com/en/About-Us/What-Is-Esports.html

Antolín, R., Reyes, A., & Ruiz, N. (2021). Explorando los factores que afectan al comportamiento de los consumidores en plataformas de live streaming. *Revista Espacios*, *42*(14). https://doi.org/10.48082/espacios-a21v42n14p03

Antón, M., & García, F. (2014). Deportes electrónicos. Una aproximación a las posibilidades comunicativas de un mercado emergente. *Questiones Publicitarias, 1*(19), 98–115. https://doi.org/10.5565/rev/qp.28

Bartle, A. (2003). *Designing virtual worlds.* Indianapolis: New Riders Games.

Bosman, S. (2019). Women account for 46% of all game enthusiasts: watching game video content and esports has changed how women and men alike engage with games. https://newzoo.com/insights/articles/women-account-for-46-of-all-game-enthusiasts-watching-game-video-content-and-esports-has-changed-how-women-and-men-alike-engage-with-games/

Brown Kramer, J., Sabalka, L., Rush, B., Jones, K., & Nolte, T. (2020, June). Automated depth video monitoring for fall reduction: a case study. In *Proceedings of the IEEE/CVF Conference on Computer Vision and Pattern Recognition (CVPR) Workshops* (pp. 16–18), Seattle, WI: Institute of Electrical and Electronics Engineers.

Caro, J. (2021). *Esports: un horizonte de beneficios de mercadeo para las marcas en Colombia Motivaciones, necesidades y beneficios del eSports Marketing* [Bachelor's thesis]. Universidad EAFIT. https://bit.ly/3iMHfiU

Carrillo, J. (2016). De jugadores a espectadores La construcción del espectáculo mediático en el contexto de los e-sports. *Anàlisi: quaderns de comunicació i cultura, 55,* 1–16. https://doi.org/10.7238/a.v0i55.2893

González, E. (2021). Streaming en tiempo real para eventos deportivos. Las redes sociales como estrategia de difusión de contenidos [Bachelor's thesis]. Universidad de Palermo. https://bit.ly/3lrZ2O8

Graf, D. L., Pratt, L. V., & Hester, C. N. (2009). Jugar con viojuegos activos aumenta el gasto de energía de los niños. *Pediatrics, 68*(2), 70.

Gutiérrez-Serafín, B., Pérez-Espinosa, H., Espinosa-Curiel, I., Figueroa-García, P., Pozas-Bogarín, E., & Martínez-Miranda, J. (2019). Estimación automática del gasto energético de la actividad física de niños en videojuegos de ejercicio con el sensor Kinect. *Research in Computing Science, 148*(8), 263–277.

Jiménez, J. M., & Araya, Y. C. (2012). El efecto de los videojuegos en variables sociales, psicológicas y fisiológicas en niños y adolescentes. *Retos. Nuevas tendencias en Educación Física, deporte y recreación, 21,* 43–49.

Kelly, K. (1993). The first online sports game. Netrek is Mind Hockey on the Net. https://www.wired.com/1993/06/netrek/

Marín, B. (2021). Streaming: ventajas, desafíos y oportunidades de las radio-televisiones para captar audiencias. *Revista de Ciencias de la Comunicación e Información, 26,* 45–65. https://bit.ly/3aocmg1

Márquez, R. (2017). Las universidades americanas ya ofrecen becas deportivas a jugadores. eSports. Xataka Esports, 1, 1. https://bit.ly/2wjej93

Pellegrini, A. (2011). *The Oxford handbook of the development of play.* Oxford University Press.

Pérez, M. (2019). *El gasto energético en sesiones con videojuegos activos.* [Tesis de Grado]. *Facultad de Ciencias Físicas y del deporte.* Universidad de Zaragoza.

Rodríguez, J., Abad, M., & Giménez, F. (2009). Concepto, características, orientaciones y clasificaciones del deporte actual. *Revista Digital efdeportes. com, 138.* https://www.efdeportes.com/efd138/concepto-y-clasificaciones-del-deporte-actual.htm

Rodríguez, M. (2017). *El tratamiento informativo de los eSports como especialización periodística deportiva en España* [Bachelor's thesis]. Universidad de Sevilla. https://bit.ly/2WZ4ajl

Romo, L. (2017). *Revolución digital: el caso de los deportes electrónicos en los medios de comunicación deportivos* [Bachelor's thesis]. Universidad Autónoma de Barcelona. https://bit.ly/3DuyBxw

Scheuerl, H. (1994). *Das Spiel. Untersuchungen über sein wesen, seine pädagogischen möglichkeiten und grenzen.* Beltz Verlag.

Toro, S. (2021). Juego y motricidad, ludanzando en el existir. In S. Toro & J. Vega (Eds.), *Manifestaciones de la Motricidad Humana, brotes desde el sur* (pp. 97–128). Valdivia: Ediciones Uach.

Trotter, M. G., Coulter, T. J., Davis, P. A., Poulus, D. R., & Polman, R. (2020). The association between esports participation, health and physical activity behaviour. *International Journal of Environmental Research and Public Health, 17,* 7329. https://doi.org/10.3390/ijerph17197329

Varona, D. (2018). Streaming: la sociedad broadcast. In C. Obando & J. Hernández (Eds.), *La metafísica de internet* (pp. 142–166). Universidad San Jorge de Zaragoza. https://bit.ly/3AzcgN7

4 Marketing Strategies for Esports

Sonia Esther González-Moreno, Jesús Manuel Palma-Ruiz, and Luis Ever Caro-Lazos

Introduction

Esports can be defined as competitive video gaming and has become a worldwide phenomenon with exponential growth among many nations. Esports is a lucrative industry (Santos et al., 2021) that flourished rapidly during 2020 and 2021 due to pandemic lockdown regulations (Ke & Wagner, 2020). The industry reported close to $1.1 billion in revenue in 2019, and it is projected to reach up to $2.3 billion by 2024, generating as much revenue as other professional sports, such as Formula 1 (1.8 billion) and the UEFA Champions League (2.26 billion) (Gough, 2021b; Green Man Gaming, 2022). In addition, with more than 474 million global viewers in 2021, esports surpassed the 410 million audience for American Football, and in 2024 it is expected to reach 577 million viewers (Newzoo, 2021). In fact, live viewership jumped from 15.3 million hours in 2018 to 98.5 million in 2019 in mobile esports – an increase of more than 600% (Newzoo, 2020). Besides, the number of professional players more than tripled going from 8k in 2012 to 25k in 2019, and this trend is expected to continue in the upcoming years (Newzoo, 2019; Palma-Ruiz et al., 2022). For example, a report on the USA Gaming Industry stated that 53.1% of the US population were to be considered monthly gamers by the end of 2021, considering a modest 1.1% annual growth from the 5.7% increase observed from 2019 to 2020 (Droesch, 2021).

The implication of such growth is massive in terms of market trends and business opportunities of all sorts. Recent studies on esports have addressed the impact of COVID-19 lockdown regulations on brand extension (Ke & Wagner, 2020), advertising in the games (Quilliam et al., 2011), flow experience (Ham et al., 2016), brand exposure (Gawrysiak et al., 2020), and consumption motives including media offerings (Ji & Hanna, 2020). Acquiring supportive information that focuses on consumer loyalty, motivations, and consumption behaviors within

DOI: 10.4324/9781003273691-7

esports could assist stakeholders in this industry to define marketing management methods. This is important for marketing strategies and other techniques, which will help categorize the heterogeneous esports consumer base when pushing marketing initiatives (Santos et al., 2021).

The aim of this chapter is to identify and compare the marketing strategies and techniques that are carried out among the top-five ranking esports teams around the globe by describing the official websites. Moreover, we record the changes in the number of followers within the main social media platforms used by such teams over a five-month period. This chapter is organized as follows. The next section includes an overview of the current esports situation in terms of legitimization of the sports and a discussion of the esports ecosystem in terms of content, brand exposure, merchandise, and subscriptions. Section 3 presents the methodology, and Section 4 describes the main results. Finally, Section 5 concludes with implications for practice and recommendations for future studies.

Legitimization of Esports

Esports is a growing industry that engages in all the economic activities associated with traditional sports. Years before, Crawford & Gosling (2009) had already commented that esports required the same skill training and development, interpersonal competition, and dexterity as ordinary sports. Moreover, esports are inserted into regional and international competition, organized around teams' management, including training and practice, and treatment of physical injuries and psychological stress of players (Fiore et al., 2020).

Additional support to consider esports as sports comes from the academic and economic standpoints. On the one hand, studies suggest that when considering the mental and physical skills required to compete professionally, these online games should be qualified as a sport (Funk et al., 2018). In fact, since the emphasis of the game switched from person against computer to people versus others, the attention in the gaming industry increased significantly due to this new competition environment (Griffiths et al., 2003). As a result, when online gaming activities began to become popular, some scholars and industry professionals argued against considering it a sport. For instance, in 2014, the president of ESPN – a well-known global sports broadcasting company based in the USA – declared: "It's not a sport – it's a competition" (Tassi, 2014). However, more opinions have been posited regarding its consideration as a sport. For example, in 2015, *Sports Illustrated* – a leading US magazine in sports – published "E-sports nation: How competitive gaming became a flourishing sport" acknowledging esports as sports (Apstein, 2015).

On the other hand, in a specialized summit conducted in 2017, the International Olympic Committee (IOC) recognized "the rapid growth of competitive video gaming as well as the potential for future applications of AR/VR technologies in esports and gaming" (British Esports Association, 2019, para. 3). In this vein, in 2018, an Esports Forum was hosted at the Olympic Museum in Switzerland, where the IOC and the Global Association of International Sports Federations began conversations regarding esports. The event was an important episode in the industry since it started conversations regarding areas of "commonality and potential collaboration, including the question of whether esports could be recognized as a sport... (and) be represented within the Olympic Movement" (International Olympic Committee, 2018, para. 3).

In 2021, the IOC along with five international sports federations and game publishers organized the first Olympic Virtual Series (OVS); the competitions took place from May 13 to June 23 and included virtual sailing, cycling, rowing, motorsports, and baseball (International Olympic Committee, 2021a, para. 2). The OVS represented "the first-ever Olympic-licensed event for... non-physical virtual sports" as stated by the IOC. Thomas Bach, president of the IOC, commented that the objective of the event was to engage younger audiences in sports participation and the promotion of Olympic values (International Olympic Committee, 2021b). This is an important statement from IOC to acknowledge esports into future games and the "legitimization" of the sports.

In September 2021, the IOC announced the debut of esports on Asian Games 2022, where competitors will finally be able to acknowledge their triumphs with gold, silver, and bronze medals. The selected FIFA games (made by EA Sports, a worldwide developer and distributor of digital entertainment) are Arena of Valor, Dota 2, Dream Three Kingdoms 2, FIFA soccer, Hearthstone, League of Legends, PUBG Mobile, and Street Fighter V (Venkat, 2021).

Throughout the years, esports have been permeating as a legitimate sport in society, ultimately gaining territory and being acknowledged not only by sports authorities but supported by the different key stakeholders and key players in the value chain industry.

Esports ecosystem and marketing strategies

Some of the most promising and latest areas for the study of marketing strategy and consumer behavior relate to shifting the focus back to the customer (Sheth, 2021). On the one hand, the study on creating value for customers and brand value are recognized as new frontiers of research in the field of marketing strategy. Customers are looking for both service and performance value. In esports, customers look for valuable experiences both as users and as buyers. Some of these experiences are in part given away to a certain extent by each of the key stakeholders in a complex esports ecosystem. The success of esports relates to the increasing interest, experience, and maturity of such key players in the ecosystem. Consumers, teams, professional players/influencers, sponsors/advertisers, broadcasting platforms, and organizers comprise the esports ecosystem and represent key stakeholders in the industry's value chain (Carrillo Vera & Aguado Terrón, 2019; Saiz-Alvarez et al., 2021).

On the other hand, a promising area for the study of consumer behavior relates to the user experience and engagement. Such interest is mainly due to the growth of social media. Esports have outstripped traditional sports by adopting the Internet as its mainstay, while integrating a collection of thrilling changes to its content production and delivery, exploiting, and consolidating new media techniques and processes, such as live streaming and content through social media, websites, blogs, and video platforms (i.e., Twitch, Twitter, YouTube, Facebook, Discord, VK, TikTok, Weibo) (Block et al., 2018; Saiz-Alvarez et al., 2021). Most of esports consumption occurs through platforms such as Twitch and YouTube (Jenny et al., 2018).

Esports have embraced many characteristics of ordinary sports such as professional athletes (and its respective well-organized teams and sponsorships), organizers, such as governed associations and leagues, media coverage, or broadcasting platforms (Jenny et al., 2017), and distinctive consumers or spectators (Cranmer et al., 2021). Figure 4.1 shows the esports ecosystem in terms of content, brand exposure, merchandise, and subscriptions.

As esports teams are maturing and expanding into different disciplines, consumer groups from diverse generations, including players, fans, and viewers, are becoming even more drawn into them, proving to be not only a money-spinning alternative profession for many, but a highly entertaining substitute to traditional sports (Qian, Wang, et al., 2020). As a result, teams are becoming even more professionalized than ever. There are all sorts of marketing strategies and techniques to attract more followers and appeal to different audiences; social media, digital channels, special events, sponsorships, and merchandising are just a few examples. The growing audience and diverse consumer

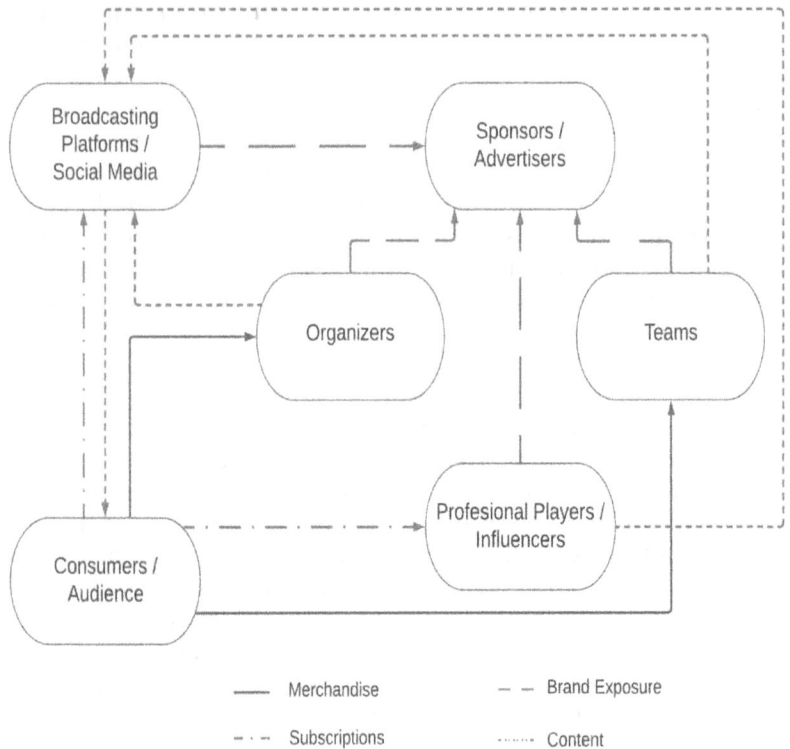

Figure 4.1 Esports ecosystem. Adapted from Newzoo (2021)

markets have drawn global corporate sponsors as well, such as Microsoft, Samsung, and Red Bull (Funk et al., 2018).

In this regard, esports' attractiveness has been greatly motivated by the active involvement of the audience, including schedule convenience, virtual rewards, chat room interactions with professional players and influencers, embracing streamer characters, which are unique characteristics and set them apart from traditional sports (Qian, Zhang, et al., 2020).

These motivators have been reported by other scholars to be correlated with consumption behavior, thus leading to loyalty and connection between teams, players, and fans (Jenny et al., 2018; Kim & Trail, 2010). Another important driver of esports consumption refers to vicarious achievement, or the emotions linked to the connection between fans and their teams (Qian, Wang, et al., 2020). Social interaction is one of the main contributors to esport consumption (Hamari & Sjöblom, 2017). Other studies found the attainment of knowledge from amateur players to be related to team loyalty as well (Santos et al., 2021).

Esports teams collect revenues from several venues, such as sponsorships, tournaments and prizes, merchandise and tickets, media rights, and streaming. In 2021, implications of esports consumer spending resulted in merchandise acquisition for over $121.7 million, while $116.3 million was derived from sponsorships, via tournaments, partnerships, and organizers (Newzoo, 2020). Also, $833.6 million in revenues resulted from media rights and sponsorships. These revenue streams alone will exceed $1.6 to 2.3 billion by 2024 (Gough, 2021b; Green Man Gaming, 2022; Newzoo, 2020).

The top-ranking teams, as of June 2021, as per earnings and accumulated money prizes, are depicted on Table 4.1 with an analysis based on Statista and esportsearnings.com.

Based on Statista data, as of November 2021, Team Spirit (Russia) occupied the fourth place, and Fnatic (UK) climbed down to sixth place. Moreover, based on esportsearnings.com, as of February 2022, Team Spirit (Russia) occupied fourth place, Virtus.pro (Russia) fifth place, Natus Vincere (Ukraine) sixth place, and Fnatic (UK) seventh place.

Table 4.1 Top-ranking esports teams, earnings, and accumulated money prizes

Rank	Team	Statista		esportsearnings.com	
		Earnings in US dollars as of June 2021	Earnings in US dollars as of Nov. 2021	Accumulated money prizes in US dollars as of June 2021	Accumulated money prizes in US dollars as of Feb. 2022
1	Team Liquid (Europe)	$36,700,000	$37,820,000	$37,560,627	$38,476,764
2	OG (Europe)	$34,420,000	$35,630,000	$34,550,723	$35,702,823
3	Evil Geniuses (USA)	$24,470,000	$25,520,000	$24,668,338	$25,589,757
4	Fnatic (UK)	$16,060,000	$17,300,000	$16,327,055	$17,496,548
5	Virtus.pro (Russia)	$15,750,000	$17,750,000	$16,056,141	$18,152,325

Source: Esports Earnings (2021), Gough (2021a), and Petermeier (2020)

Methodology

This research is of qualitative nature with an explorative and descriptive scope. In the first part of this study, we employed a website analysis technique. Content analysis refers to one of the most used research methods in social sciences and is recognized as a systematic and objective means to quantify specific phenomena and to analyze data within a specific context to make valid inferences from verbal, visual, or written data (Bowen, 2009). Content analysis is used as a qualitative research technique to understand the content of print publications, websites, and social media pages and groups (Hsieh & Shannon, 2005).

Considering the information on Table 4.1, we analyzed the official websites of the top-ranking esports teams to gain insights into the site organization, and the main perceived marketing strategies and approaches that showed the transmission of content, brand exposure, merchandise, and subscriptions, while, at the same time, to sense the connections between teams, players, and customers/audience. The analysis took place from September 1 to 10, 2021. The second part of this study consisted in recording a change in the number of followers in the main common social media platforms of the same top-five ranking esports teams (as shown in Table 4.1), over a five-month difference. Data records were taken on September 9, 2021, and February 9, 2022. Such data allows the authors to partially capture the effect of those strategies over such a period and to make some inferences. In the following section, a description of the most notable findings resulting from the website analysis is described, and Table 4.2 includes a summary of the main marketing elements identified.

Results

Team Liquid (https://teamliquid.com)

The Team Liquid website is static and organized into different sections; these include News, For Fans, Players, Partners, Store, About, and Careers. At the very top of the home page, visitors can find the Alienware sponsor logo. Links to eight main platforms and social media are included, such as YouTube, Twitter, Instagram, Facebook, and VK. On the home page, a game schedule for the following seven days is included, in addition to a Twitter addon that shows the most recent postings (including followers). Further down the main page, news and stories about their players and teams are shown, including a short summary and photograph. Interestingly, Team Liquid has launched Liquid+ for fans to follow their favorite Liquid players, games, streamers. This app available for Apple and Android devices is based on engagement and point rewards. Liquid+ connects the user's social media and tracks every posting, hashtag, emoji, cheer, tweet related to Team Liquid. Those points can be exchanged later for merchandise and other prizes (such as signed jerseys). The Liquid Store includes a broad apparel and featured collection, including championship jerseys. Models used in the store are the actual Liquid players, who also promote their own apparel collections.

OG (https:/logs.ggl)

The OG website is animated and divided into sections, such as About OG esports, Shop, News, Teams, Staff, Community, Partners, and Contact. Links to eight main platforms and social media are included, like Twitter, Facebook, Instagram, YouTube, TikTok, VK, Weibo, and Discord. A banner occupying about 80% of the Welcome home screen shows an invitation to read more About OG esports and to check out the merchandise (showing a photograph of main OG players as models). The lower section of the home page shows the logos of their main sponsors, including RedBull, Fun88, BMW, Steelseries, socios.com, Secretlab, Wintermute, and IC markets. Below the sponsors, a collection of videos (True Sight) with insights about the players, teams, experiences, and final tournaments are included. A list of achievements containing the name of the tournament and the place position attained is also shown. The Teams section includes Dota, CS:GO, and Valorant, with short players' biographies and game positions. The OG Store offers apparel, accessories, and athletics. The community section uses a Discord addon and shows the current members online; in addition, fans can share and submit their artwork in this section. Further down the main page, news about their players and teams are also shown, including YouTube videos, photographs, and other social media links.

Evil Geniuses (https:/levilgeniuses.ggl)

The Evil Geniuses (EG) site is organized into the following sections: About, Schedule, Teams, Partners, Programs, News, and Store. The main Welcome page shows their big EG logo and below a collage of photographs of players, teams, and events. The schedule is right below, followed by the different EG teams. A short biography of each of the players and a photograph is shown within each game. The logos of their partners are all included in a mobile banner and are linked to their corresponding websites, such as Monster Energy, Ultra Gear, Absolute, Bud Light, Elysian Brewing, Secret Lab, Tumi, Bitcasino.io, Peak6, Point3, Wolves Football Club (FC). The EG history contains a year timeline of achievements and relevant news, such as tournament championships, acquisitions, and partnerships. The EG Store offers apparel and accessories, including special collections with their partners' branding. For example, Secretlab and EG teamed up to offer gaming chairs' year series in different sizes and upholsteries. Wolves FC from the UK Soccer Premier League and EG joined forces to offer fan jerseys, stickers, and other accessories. A Live Proud collection appealing to the LGBT community is available. Newsletter subscriptions' popups show on different occasions while visiting the Store, as well as links to subscribe for content for EG and their partners. It is noted that the EG Site is compliant with the Americans with Disabilities Act Standards for accessible design (ADA). Within the Programs section, users can find Factor.gg, which is an EG spin-off for advanced statistics in esports with the mission to "redefine the way professional esports is watched, analyzed, and talked about through the use of data and advanced statistics". Interestingly, EG is actively involved with different groups in the community; for example, programs focused on women in gaming, such as Pokerpower, Black Girls Code, PressForward. Additional EG partnerships with organizations such as Cxmmunity and YouGov exist to increase the minority youth participation and explore the effects of gaming in the industry, respectively. The LiveProud Podcast is another program designed to share and discuss issues via Spotify and YouTube for the LGBT community around the globe. Other partnership initiatives include supporting people within their organization through Live Evil & Live Well, and the Gamers Outreach, a non-profit foundation to support hospitalized children. Links to their social media platforms (eight) are at the very bottom of their site.

Fnatic (https://fnatic.com/)

Fnatic site is structured into four main sections: Esports, Products, Company, and Shop. At the top of the Welcome page, visitors can find a Twitch addon showing the live games, players, and teams online, followed by the current number of viewers, where visitors can also join with a click. Immediately below, occupying the center of the page, a mixture of sections including, news, collaborations with partners, and products advertisement is shown, such as new apparel and gear. Further down, links to the four most recent gaming videos in YouTube are displayed, followed by Fnatic Gear, such as keyboards, mouses, headsets, mousepads, PCs & chairs, accessories, among others, in addition to apparel and new lines of products. Models used for the shop are actual players of the Fnatic team. An interesting program refers to the Fnatic Network, where influencers can subscribe to increase their audience, improve their game, meet with players, other users, and influencers, and earn rewards based on tiers for growth (including social reach, hours of streamed content, Twitch concurrent viewers per stream or ccu). Newsletter subscription is available at the bottom of the homepage, where the partners' logos and links to their sites are shown, such as asos, BMW, crypto.com, Monster Energy, Jack Link's, L'Oréal Men Expert, Hisense, Anda Seat, letou.com, and Kaspersky. Within the Esports section, the different teams are classified per game; listings for upcoming and past games are displayed, in addition to information of each player, including a short biography, photograph, and individual social media links. Also, the player's picks in apparel and gear are advertised and linked to the Fnatic Shop. The Company section includes highlights of achievements referring to tournaments, players, earnings, social fans, facilities, and staff members, among others. In terms of branding, Fnatic underline their collaboration with GUCCI, described as "the first tie-up between an esports team and a true luxury powerhouse". Details about other partnerships are included in the News subsection under Company, such as Nielsen Sports and Entertainment, featuring a whitepaper on Return on Investment (ROI) on esports. Finally, at the bottom of the homepage, Fnatic links to the main social media platforms are included, such as Twitter, Twitch, YouTube, Instagram, TikTok, Facebook, Discord, and Github.

Virtus.pro (https://virtus.pro/)

Virtus.pro site includes seven main sections, including News, Teams, Matches, Results, Shop, About, and Fan Center. Top news is displayed at the Welcome page, followed by a schedule for the upcoming three games. A section of featured videos (YouTube) with interviews with players (most, if not all, are recorded in Russian with English subtitles) are included below. Instagram and Twitter addons follow the videos section, including latest publications of the team. Limited apparel and gear are available through the Shop, including other accessories such as Kingston Fury PC memory (partner). Interestingly, a Virtus.pro app for fans called Bearloga is available for Apple and Android devices. This app allows direct communication among fans, players, and club management, and to receive up-to-date information about game schedule, players, and line-ups, in addition to unique content, results, and voting influencing the decisions of the club. Links to Virtus.pro main partners' websites is shown at the bottom of the homepage, including Winline, Hyper, Haval, Bybit, Kingston Fury, Metro, SbertMarket. Finally, a summary of followers per each social media platform is shown, such as Facebook, VK, YouTube, Instagram, Twitter, Telegram, and TikTok. Within the Teams section, teams are classified per game; listings for upcoming matches and results are displayed, in addition to information of each player, including a short biography, photograph, and his social media links. Unfortunately, the Partnership subsection under About was under construction, and some other page errors (404) were present in the site.

As shown in Table 4.2, the top-ranking esports teams follow in many aspects similar marketing strategies, particularly by being extremely active on social media platforms. In terms of transmission of content, besides the actual social media platforms and websites, Team Liquid and Virtus.pro stand out from the others by offering a free mobile app to connect, share content, and engage with their fans. Yet, EG has developed factor.gg for advanced statistics and analytics in esports, allowing their fans to advance their gaming experience. On the other hand, the Fnatic Network is a clear attempt to support players to become influencers and extend the Fnatic content globally. Finally, OG uses a more traditional YouTube media through a collection of professionally enhanced videos labeled as True Sight to share new content about their players, tournaments, wins, and behind the scenes experiences. In terms of brand exposure, all esports teams are active on social media. Unlike the others, EG seems particularly focused on diversity and inclusive participation, including programs, community initiatives, and partnerships with organizations, involving women, minorities, LGBT, and other groups. Related to merchandising, all teams offer their own apparel, gear, and accessories. However, Fnatic and EG seem to have capitalized to a greater extent their partnerships to broaden their collections of products and to offer special editions with both brands. Fnatic and GUCCI, or EG and Secretlab, for example, offer gaming chairs in different sizes and upholsteries, while EG and Wolves FC offer fan jerseys with both of their logos. It is clear that new corporate partners and sponsors are entering the esports industry and appear to select the most well-positioned teams in the ranking. Examples of partners and sponsors include Alienware, Red-Bull, Fun88, BMW, Secretlab, Monster Energy, Ultra Gear, Absolute, Bud Light, Wolves FC, crypto.com, L'Oréal Men Expert, Hisense, Kaspersky, Kingston Fury, among many others.

Table 4.2 Summary of main top-five ranking esports marketing strategies and techniques

Rank	Team	Transmission of content	Brand exposure	Merchandising	Subscriptions
1	Team Liquid	Liquid+ App and point rewards	Social media (8)	Liquid Store (broad apparel, special collections)	Liquid+ App, social media, and newsletter
2	OG (Europe)	True Sight videos	Social media (8)	OG Shop (limited apparel)	Social media
3	Evil Geniuses (USA)	Factor.gg	Social media (8), diversified programs and community initiatives	EG Store (broad apparel, special collections, partnerships)	Factor.gg, social media, and newsletter
4	Fnatic (UK)	Fnatic Network and tier rewards	Social media (8) and Network	Fnatic Shop (broad apparel, gear, partnerships)	Fnatic Network, social media, and newsletter
5	Virtus.pro (Russia)	Bearloga App	Social media (7) and App	Virtus.pro Shop (limited apparel)	Bearloga App and social media

Source: The Authors

Table 4.3 Changes in the number of social media followers per esport team

Team	Twitter			Facebook			Instagram			YouTube		
	09/09/21	09/02/22	Dif (%)	09/09/21	09/02/22	Dif (%)	09/09/21	09/02/22	Dif (%)	09/09/21	09/02/22	Dif (%)
Team Liquid	713,957	742,262	3.96	803,904	805,321	0.18	1,003,217	1,065,257	6.18	473,000	498,000	5.29
OG	708,248	781,194	10.30	597,361	867,793	45.27	364,044	385,103	5.78	55,700	80,200	43.99
Evil Geniuses	567,326	589,598	3.93	467,280	487,097	4.24	202,031	208,173	3.04	117,000	118,000	0.85
Fnatic	1,573,827	1,613,224	2.50	2,474,778	2,443,958	-1.25	1,202,880	1,235,668	2.73	719,000	722,000	0.42
Virtus.pro	247,680	260,458	5.16	462,051	459,006	-0.66	344,042	341,644	-0.70	314,000	309,000	-1.59

Source: Twitter, Facebook, Instagram, and YouTube

The results for the second part of this study refer to the changes in social media followers per esports teams over a five-month difference (see Table 4.3).

Based on Table 4.3, notable changes during this period occurred with regard to OG, such as an increase in their Facebook followers by more than 45%, YouTube subscribers by more than 43%, Twitter followers by more than 10%, and Instagram followers by more than 5%. Fnatic Facebook followers decreased by 1.25%, and Facebook, Instagram, and YouTube followers too decreased for Virtus.pro during this period. Team Liquid and EG remained positive with an overall increase in their social media platforms. Interestingly, OG followers increased on YouTube, which can be inferred from their efforts to exploit True Sight videos as their marketing strategy, as shown in Table 4.2.

Conclusions

The esports industry has continued to be legitimized over the years and it has been confirmed as a worldwide phenomenon with relevant financial, political, and social implications, particularly for the stakeholders involved in its value chain. Top-ranking esports teams have become full-grown and are being managed as professionally as many traditional sports teams, including sponsorships, partnerships, branding management, product placement, and marketing strategies, to name a few. This study shows the extent of the use of marketing strategies to identify and compare those related to the transmission of content, brand exposure, merchandise, and subscriptions by the top-five ranking esports teams in the world. Our results demonstrate in part the relevance of sponsorships sought by teams through corporate partners to increase their merchandise assortment, special editions, and collections, for market penetration and brand exposure. Future studies should look deeply into the teams' revenues per merchandise and advertisement in different settings and contexts and compare the individual impact of social media platforms, tournaments, special events, and community programs. Moreover, the development of new means of content and the ability to successfully transmit it to their fans to increase their loyalty and engagement appear decisive in ensuring their esports market positioning and to increase their revenues. Future studies should consider the specific impact of esports fan apps and rewards systems (such as Liquid+ or Bearloga App) and the fan loyalty and engagement versus more traditional social media platforms. In addition, new monetization methods, non-fungible tokens, and other rewards or fan investment into teams are worth exploring. While results in this study showed a positive increase in social media followers for all the esports teams, in some cases a decrease was also noted. Other relevant variables should be analyzed during the period of study, such as players signing or team switching, tournament results that may also influence the fans' preferences and team loyalty. Figure 4.1 Esports ecosystem. Adapted from Newzoo (2021)

References

Apstein, S. (2015). *E-sports nation: how competitive gaming became a flourishing sport*. Sports Illustrated. https://www.si.com/more-sports/2015/10/29/esports-competitive-video-gaming

Block, F., Hodge, V., Hobson, S., Sephton, N., Devlin, S., Ursu, M. F., Drachen, A., & Cowling, P. I. (2018). Narrative bytes: data-driven content production in esports. In *Proceedings of the 2018 ACM International Conference on Interactive Experiences for TV and Online Video* (pp. 29–41). https://doi.org/10.1145/3210825.3210833

Bowen, G. A. (2009). Document analysis as a qualitative research method. *Qualitative Research Journal, 9*(2), 27–40. https://doi.org/10.3316/QRJ0902027

British Esports Association. (2019). *IOC interview: 'esports can be a fantastic way to promote Olympic values'*. British Esports. https://britishesports.org/interviews/ioc-esports-olympics-interview/

Carrillo Vera, J. A., & Aguado Terrón, J. M. (2019). The eSports ecosystem: stakeholders and trends in a new show business. *Catalan Journal of Communication & Cultural Studies, 11*(1), 3–22. https://doi.org/10.1386/cjcs.11.1.3_1

Cranmer, E. E., Han, D.-I. D., van Gisbergen, M., & Jung, T. (2021). Esports matrix: structuring the esports research agenda. *Computers in Human Behavior, 117*, 106671. https://doi.org/10.1016/j.chb.2020.106671

Crawford, G., & Gosling, V. K. (2009). More than a game: sports-themed video games and player narratives. *Sociology of Sport Journal, 26*(1), 50–66. https://doi.org/10.1123/ssj.26.1.50

Droesch, B. (2021). *The US gaming ecosystem 2021*. Insider Intelligence. https://www.emarketer.com/content/us-gaming-ecosystem-2021

Esports Earnings. (2021). *Team rankings*. Esports Earnings. https://www.esportsearnings.com/teams

Fiore, R., Zampaglione, D., Murazzi, E., Bucchieri, F., Cappello, F., & Fucarino, A. (2020). The eSports conundrum: is the sports sciences community ready to face them? A perspective. *The Journal of Sports Medicine and Physical Fitness, 60*(12). https://doi.org/10.23736/S0022-4707.20.10892-2

Funk, D. C., Pizzo, A. D., & Baker, B. J. (2018). eSport management: embracing eSport education and research opportunities. *Sport Management Review, 21*(1), 7–13. https://doi.org/10.1016/j.smr.2017.07.008

Gawrysiak, J., Burton, R., Jenny, S., & Williams, D. (2020). Using esports efficiently to enhance and extend brand perceptions-a literature review. *Physical Culture and Sport, Studies and Research, 86*(1), 1–14. https://doi.org/10.2478/pcssr-2020-0008

Gough, C. (2021a). *All time highest-winning pro eSports teams worldwide 2021.* Statista. https://www.statista.com/statistics/954410/highest-winning-esports-team/

Gough, C. (2021b). *eSports market revenue worldwide from 2019 to 2024.* Statista. https://www.statista.com/statistics/490522/global-esports-market-revenue/

Green Man Gaming. (2022). *Esports—the money game.* Green Man Gaming. https://www.greenmangaming.com/the-money-game/

Griffiths, M. D., Davies, M. N. O., & Chappell, D. (2003). Breaking the stereotype: the case of online gaming. *CyberPsychology & Behavior, 6*(1), 81–91. https://doi.org/10.1089/109493103321167992

Ham, C.-D., Yoon, G., & Nelson, M. R. (2016). The interplay of persuasion inference and flow experience in an entertaining food advergame. *Journal of Consumer Behaviour, 15*(3), 239–250. https://doi.org/10.1002/cb.1564

Hamari, J., & Sjöblom, M. (2017). What is eSports and why do people watch it? *Internet Research, 27*(2), 211–232. https://doi.org/10.1108/IntR-04-2016-0085

Hsieh, H.-F., & Shannon, S. E. (2005). Three approaches to qualitative content analysis. *Qualitative Health Research, 15*(9), 1277–1288. https://doi.org/10.1177/1049732305276687

International Olympic Committee. (2018). *Olympic movement, esports and gaming communities meet at the Esports Forum.* IOC News. https://olympics.com/ioc/news/olympic-movement-esports-and-gaming-communities-meet-at-the-esports-forum

International Olympic Committee. (2021a). *Inaugural Olympic virtual series concludes successfully.* IOC News. https://olympics.com/ioc/news/inaugural-olympic-virtual-series-concludes-successfully

International Olympic Committee. (2021b). *IOC makes landmark move into virtual sports by announcing first-ever Olympic Virtual Series.* IOC News. https://olympics.com/ioc/news/international-olympic-committee-makes-landmark-move-into-virtual-sports-by-announcing-first-ever-olympic-virtual-series

Jenny, S. E., Keiper, M. C., Taylor, B. J., Williams, D. P., Gawrysiak, J., Manning, R. D., & Tutka, P. M. (2018). eSports venues: a new sport business opportunity. *Journal of Applied Sport Management, 10*(1), 34–49. https://doi.org/10.18666/JASM-2018-V10-I1-8469

Jenny, S. E., Manning, R. D., Keiper, M. C., & Olrich, T. W. (2017). Virtual(ly) athletes: where eSports fit within the definition of "sport". *Quest, 69*(1), 1–18. https://doi.org/10.1080/00336297.2016.1144517

Ji, Z., & Hanna, R. C. (2020). Gamers first – how consumer preferences impact esports media offerings. *International Journal on Media Management, 22*(1), 13–29. https://doi.org/10.1080/14241277.2020.1731514

Ke, X., & Wagner, C. (2020). Global pandemic compels sport to move to esports: understanding from brand extension perspective. *Managing Sport and Leisure, July,* 1–6. https://doi.org/10.1080/23750472.2020.1792801

Kim, Y. K., & Trail, G. (2010). Constraints and motivators: a new model to explain sport consumer behavior. *Journal of Sport Management, 24*(2), 190–210. https://doi.org/10.1123/jsm.24.2.190

Newzoo. (2019). *Global esports market 2017–2019*. Newzoo. https://newzoo.com/insights/trend-reports/newzoo-global-esports-market-report-2019-light-version/

Newzoo.(2020).*2020Globalesportsmarketreport*.Newzoo.https://newzoo.com/insights/trend-reports/newzoo-global-esports-market-report-2020-light-version/

Newzoo. (2021). *Global esports & live streaming market report*. Newzoo. https://newzoo.com/insights/trend-reports/newzoos-global-esports-live-streaming-market-report-2021-free-version/

Palma-Ruiz, J. M., Torres-Toukoumidis, A., González-Moreno, S. E., & Valles-Baca, H. G. (2022). An overview of the gaming industry across nations: using analytics with power BI to forecast and identify key influencers. *Heliyon, 8*(2), e08959. https://doi.org/10.1016/j.heliyon.2022.e08959

Petermeier,D.(2020).*Top5: themostsuccessfuleSportsteamsintheworld*.ISPO.Com https://www.ispo.com/en/trends/top-5-most-successful-esports-teams-world

Qian, T. Y., Wang, J. J., Zhang, J. J., & Lu, L. Z. (2020). It is in the game: dimensions of esports online spectator motivation and development of a scale. *European Sport Management Quarterly, 20*(4), 458–479. https://doi.org/10.108 0/16184742.2019.1630464

Qian, T. Y., Zhang, J. J., Wang, J. J., & Hulland, J. (2020). Beyond the game: dimensions of esports online spectator demand. *Communication & Sport, 8*(6), 825–851. https://doi.org/10.1177/2167479519839436

Quilliam, E. T., Lee, M., Cole, R. T., & Kim, M. (2011). The impetus for (and limited power of) business self-regulation: the example of advergames. *Journal of Consumer Affairs, 45*(2), 224–247. https://doi.org/10.1111/j.1745-6606.2011.01201.x

Saiz-Alvarez, J. M., Palma-Ruiz, J. M., Valles-Baca, H. G., & Fierro-Ramírez, L. A. (2021). Knowledge management in the esports industry: sustainability, continuity, and achievement of competitive results. *Sustainability (Switzerland), 13*(19). https://doi.org/10.3390/su131910890

Santos, R. L. dos, Petroll, M. de L. M., Boeing, R., & Scussel, F. (2021). Let's play a new game: the drivers of eSports consumption. *Research, Society and Development, 10*(5), e40710515188. https://doi.org/10.33448/rsd-v10i5.15188

Sheth, J. (2021). New areas of research in marketing strategy, consumer behavior, and marketing analytics: the future is bright. *Journal of Marketing Theory and Practice, 29*(1), 3–12. https://doi.org/10.1080/10696679.2020.1860679

Tassi, P. (2014). *ESPN boss declares eSports 'not a sport'*. Forbes. https://www.forbes.com/sites/insertcoin/2014/09/07/espn-boss-declares-esports-not-a-sport/?sh=719059da5f80

Venkat, R. (2021). *Asian games 2022: Esports to make debut; FIFA, PUBG, Dota2 among eight medal events*. InternationalOlympicCommitee. https://olympics.com/en/news/fifa-pubg-dota-2-esports-medal-events-asian-games-2022

5 Comparative Study of the Transmedia Element in Esports

America, Europe, and Asia

Gabriela Borges, Daiana Sigiliano, and Susana Costa

Introduction and state of the art

According to Newzoo 2021 reports, global esports market moved $1,084 million in 2021 (14.5% growth from 2020) with a live streaming audience of 728.8 million people (Newzoo Global Esports and Live Market Streaming Report, 2021), with about 3 billion players around the globe in 2021. China led the market with revenues of $360.1 million in 2021, followed by North America, with $243.0 million, and Western Europe, with $205.8 million. China has 92.8 million esports enthusiasts, followed by the US and Brazil, and the largest live streaming games market, with an audience of 193.0 million in 2021. In 2019, the League of Legends World Championship was the largest tournament in terms of hours of live views on Twitch and YouTube, with 105.5 million hours (Newzoo Global Games Market Report, 2021). Live content production about the games is growing, with the Just Chatting category on Twitch becoming one of the most popular, with an audience of about 1.9 billion hours live in 2020 (Newzoo Trends to Watch Report, 2021).

As a worldwide phenomenon involving young players around the world, esports present themselves as a hybrid phenomenon that considers "[...] the seamless interpenetration of media content, sport and networked information and communications technologies" (Hutchins, 2008, p. 851). In this context, Macedo and Falcão (2019, p. 3) define e-Sport "as a public sporting event practice, technologically mediated, based on competition organized among players through the incorporation of their performances", which are related to physical and cognitive skills in the use of digital technology.

Esports grew due to the enthusiasm of fan communities that began to carry out clan tournaments online and at LAN houses in the early 2000s (Wagner, 2006 *apud* Steinkuehler, 2020, p. 5). Soon corporations identified business opportunities and started offering sponsorships for the

DOI: 10.4324/9781003273691-8

events, financing of prizes, and equipment in exchange for advertising, which made the competitions more organized (Taylor, 2012).

Considering the web of relationships that are established in the development of esports in its relationship with the media, technology, entertainment, and culture, studies have been developed in different fields of knowledge, such as sociology, sports, media studies, business, computer science, law, and cognitive sciences (Reitman et al., 2020). These authors argue that various points of view aim at understanding a phenomenon that is multidisciplinary.

An important focus of the studies relates to their comparison with sports in order to understand spectatoriality. This perspective emphasizes the relationship between media and competitive game in the understanding of the community and the technology of spectatoriality that involves esports (Kaytoue et al., 2012 *apud* Reitman et al., 2020). In this sense, Taylor (2016b), supported by other authors, understands esports as "the enactment of video games as spectator-driven sport, carried out through promotional activities; broadcasting infrastructures; the socioeconomic organization of teams, tournaments, and leagues; and the embodied performances of players themselves".

Taking this into account, our research interest in this chapter focuses on the field of media studies and its possible contribution to the understanding of esports as a hybrid phenomenon. Wohn and Freeman (2020) state that it is important to understand esports as a multidimensional media ecosystem that, from the perspective of media consumption, interrelates playing, watching, spending, and live streaming. Therefore, studying the game or live streaming independently does not allow us to acquire a comprehensive understanding of how people engage in all these activities on different platforms and media. However, as a field of studies in full development, research has been developed to understand the different dynamics and tensions that are in operation in the universe of electronic sports.

In general terms, we seek to understand esports communities through live broadcasts in order to study how they are formed and how they interact with streamers (Burroughs & Rama, 2015; Hamilton et al., 2014; Kaytoue et al., 2012; Should-Allen, 2017). Wohn and Freeman (2020) point out that live broadcasts have caught the attention of scholars given their importance in the reformatting of interactive experiences, social engagement, and sense of community in online socialization spaces.

According to the Newzoo Global Games Market Report (2020), content produced by streamers, influencers, and talk shows about multiplayer battle games like Battle Royale, Fortnite (Epic Games) were seen live on Twitch, YouTube, and Mixer for 1.3 billion hours in

2019, placing the game at number one in the rankings. Successful since its launch, Fortnite had already reached more than a third of digital game streaming worldwide views on Twitch, YouTube, and Facebook platforms in May 2018 (Molla, 2018 apud Wohn & Freeman, 2020) and 78.3 million players in August, having quickly established itself as one of today's most popular games. One of the reasons for this success is its distinctive playability, through which players can destroy and build structures during battles. Fortnite's main narrative protagonists is the very fictional universe created around the game island, where each season's new events impact the environment in which Battle Royale matches are fought.

The popularity of the game among players, streamers, and spectators alike provides an excellent opportunity to try to understand which communication strategies are adopted by professional players in order to interact with their fan and viewer communities. Thus, the four best-paid Fortnite players from each continent were selected and their activities were monitored on two online platforms, Twitch and Twitter, to evaluate the way in which they operated. According to Amat (2021) and Márquez and García (2020), the Twitch and Twitter platforms cooperate mutually in discussions, engagement actions, and content production related to video games. The authors claim that the platforms cooperation can be observed in several ways, such as the repercussion on Twitter of Twitch streaming, the automation of synchronous posts, the promotion on Twitter of strategies developed on Twitch, among others.

Materials and methods

Jenson and de Castell (2018) point out that the practice of esports marks a cultural change from amateur gamer to professional player and a way of playing from being restricted to a private setting, at home, with friends, related to use value, to becoming game as work, therefore acquiring exchange value. Research (Taylor, 2015, 2016; Witkowski, 2012) has shown that most players are male, dedicated gamers and their purchasing power brings economic benefits to gaming companies and league leaders. Undoubtedly, the professionalization of esports has also led to the development of marketing, data collection, and public relations strategies to attract viewers (Taylor, 2016a; 2016b), which are an important source of esports revenue. However, the author points out that the relationship that is established between players and viewers is one of exchange and participation driven by affective relationships through the support of teams (online and offline), viewership, likes, and other forms of support (Taylor et al., 2009).

The survey of the four best-paid professional Fortnite players from America, Europe, Africa, Asia, and Oceania was based on information gathered by *Esports Earnings*.[1] The choice of the site was based on the methodology adopted by the platform, which, in addition to informing which sources were consulted in the preparation of the ranking, covering news, forum posts, interviews, team releases, and video on demand (VODs), is updated daily. After information search, carried out in September 2021, data were organized in an Excel spreadsheet with the following columns: Player Name and ID, Prize Value, Continent, Country (Nationality), Twitter Profile, Twitter Monitoring, and Twitch Profile. In this context, it is important to emphasize that the definition of continent referring to each player was based on their nationality and not on the country they resided in during the period in which this chapter was developed.

In addition to presenting interfaces and APIs (*Applications Protocol Interface*) compatible with data monitoring and extraction processes adopted in this work, as detailed below, Twitch and Twitter platforms are popular with video game players and particularly Fortnite. Thus, the choice of platforms makes it possible to discuss transmedia communication strategies adopted by professional Fortnite players.

The selection of the Twitch platform for analysis of content produced by professional Fortnite players is justified due to their strong interest in the platform. Twitch is a live streaming platform with interactive features that, despite the predominance of video game streaming, including esports competitions, also covers entertainment, sports, music, among other content. In addition to live streaming, it is also possible to post video snippets as match highlights or post in text or image format using the "about" tab, which functions as a presentation page.

Wulf et al. (2020) argue that streaming platforms like Twitch have played a key role in the growing popularity of esports, as they allow thousands of players to stream their games live daily, attract viewers, and receive donations. In addition to sharing online content, they are a source of game engagement for both players and their audience. Wulf et al. (2020, pp. 737–738) list their main characteristics as "real-time video game streaming, relationship to streaming personae and interacting with the community of users via chat". Taylor (2012) points out that video plays an important role in esports communities practice and in the creation and promotion of brands, from individual players, clans, leagues, and championships. On the other hand, chat is the main social interaction tool, as it presents several possibilities of engagement, both technical and social, and promotes a pleasant social experience. Reitman, Anderson-Coto et al. (2020) claim that Twitch and YouTube have allowed streamers to act as players and performers, as well as entertainers.

Wulf et al. (2020, p. 6) demonstrate that

> Twitch fulfils all aspects of social communities, namely, membership (by subscription to certain streamers), influence (via interaction with other viewers and the streamer), need fulfilment (they refer to rewards such as sociability, status, success, and gaining of both knowledge and skills), and emotional connection to others (through a common history and identification with others that is shaped via continuous participation). As the community has one central theme – the game and its streamer – all users join the same topic.

Twitch profile monitoring was based on API limitations, referring to low retroactive coverage and request rate limit through tokens. Thus, issues such as datification, business model, and platform governance policy only allowed for partial access to data. Therefore, exploratory monitoring of profiles on Twitch was carried out, manually collecting each publication of the players taking part in the survey.

The approach of monitoring and extracting tweets adopted in this research is part of previously developed works (Borges & Sigiliano, 2021). According to data released by Twitter (2022), in 2021, more than 2.4 billion tweets were published about games; Fortnite is among the video games with the highest rate of conversation and engagement in microblogging. The report also points out that professional players of the franchise occupy the position of most mentioned users in this social media in 2021. The selection of this social media for the analysis of content produced by players is related not only to their participation within the scope and cooperation with Twitch, but also to the model of decentralization and recentralization of data used by Twitter, facilitating access to its API. Thus, the collection of tweets, carried out between November 2020 and November 2021, was done with the help of the Python programming language. Modules such as NLTK, Jupyter, Twint, and SpaCy were also used, along with pandas and Nest_asyncio libraries for filtering, viewing, and exporting posts (Table 5.1).

After collecting data regarding Twitch and Twitter, analysis of publications was carried out, and its discussion was driven by two axes: informational architecture and content production. The first axis refers to the characteristics related to the materiality of the platforms, encompassing general and specific aspects, and the second axis is related to the contents of posts, covering theme, language, adherence to the franchise universe, and target audience.

As a video and, particularly, live streaming platform, Twitch analysis parameters cover both axes (Table 5.2).

Table 5.1 Data collection

Name of player/player ID	Prize value ($)	Continent	Country (nationality)	Twitter profile	Monitoring	Twitch profile
Kyle Giersdorf/Bugha	3,160,795.05	America	USA	@bugha	308 tweets	https://www.twitch.tv/bugha
Harrison Chang/psalm	1,873,538.80	America	USA	@psalm	628 tweets	https://www.twitch.tv/psalm
Shane Cotton/EpikWhale	1,354,667.32	America	USA	@epikwhale	207 tweets	http://www.twitch.tv/epikwhale/
Williams Aubin/Zayt	1,200,806.42	America	Canada	@zayt	337 tweets	https://www.twitch.tv/zayt/
David Wang/Aqua	1,927,524.23	Europe	Austria	@quaa	497 tweets	https://www.twitch.tv/aquav2_
Emil Bergquist Pedersen/Nyhrox	1,537,945.69	Europe	Norway	@nyhrox	460 tweets	https://www.twitch.tv/nyhrox/
Jaden Ashman/Wolfiez	1,344,978.07	Europe	UK	@wolfiez	583 tweets	https://www.twitch.tv/wolfiez
Dave Jong/Rojo	1,214,643.33	Europe	The Netherlands	@Rojo11	705 tweets	https://www.twitch.tv/rojo11
Ibrahima Kébé/napo FlyZAK	750,00	Africa	Senegal	@napo_rog	947 tweets	–
AITOUADDA Yanis/FlyZGG	2,050.00	Africa	Algeria	@FlyZGG	522 tweets	https://www.twitch.tv/flyz
–/VoltiaX	2,000.00	Africa	Egypt	@VoltiaX	355 tweets	–
Imane "Pokimane" Anys/Pokimane	36,522.51	Africa	Morocco	@imane	746 tweets	https://www.twitch.tv/pokimane
Sung Won-Je/Ming	64,100,00	Asia	South Korea	@kreofn	839 tweets	–
Lee, Jong Su/Peterpan	158,150.00	Asia	South Korea	@Peterpan_FN	301 tweets	https://www.twitch.tv/peterpan_fn
–/Maufin	96,188.80	Asia	Japan	@maufinfn	1,005 tweets	–
–/RizArt	49,208.20	Asia	Japan	@RRRIZART	977 tweets	https://www.twitch.tv/cr_rizart
Jesse Eckley/Jesse	124,235.50	Oceania	Australia	@x2twins	581 tweets	https://www.twitch.tv/x2twins
Jordan Eckley/Jordan	120,558.80	Oceania	Australia	@x2twins	581 tweets	https://www.twitch.tv/x2twins
–/Volx	116,628.80	Oceania	Australia	@volxfn	13 tweets	https://www.twitch.tv/volx
Abdullah Khudeish/Parpy	94,603.80	Oceania	New Zealand	@parpyfn	1,382 tweets	https://www.twitch.tv/parpy

In the Twitter Analysis, parameters related to informational architecture and content production were observed, covering aspects related to microblogging materiality, Fortnite universe, and player immersive experience (Table 5.3).

Table 5.2 Twitch analysis parameters

Twitch analysis parameters
Informational architecture and content production About – observes whether the page presents texts and/or fixed posts Content – reflects on multimodal elements and content in general Resources – observes which features are used by players in addition to the recorded gameplay itself Interaction – reflects how and if players interact with their followers General – observes which elements are added to the page interface, in addition to platform use frequency and posts recurrence

Table 5.3 Twitter analysis parameters

Twitter analysis parameters
Informational architecture Temporality always on – observation of interactors reinforcement of instantaneous and immediate features of Twitter in the repercussion of their posts Focus of social interaction – reflection on whether interactors stimulate and/or foster the participation of other interactors who do not follow each other, enabling the development of asymmetric connections Limitation of textual space – observes whether tweets published by interactors can systematize information and communicate effectively Indexing – reflects whether interactors post feature hashtags and how this feature is used for information segmentation Multimodal resources – observes whether interactors' publications aggregate several languages and formats such as texts, videos, GIFs, graphic representations, etc. Content production Shared media repertoire – observes whether interactors are able to create, evaluate, and analyse content based on elements that are characteristic to the community they integrate, presenting a common media repertoire Identity – reflects whether the interactor commits to the Fortnite universe, reinforcing the fictional world, the character it represents, and the immersive experience Customization – observes if the interactor gives tips, information that goes beyond that officially disclosed by the game, offering the target audience complementary content

Analysis and results

Analysis of transmedia communication strategies adopted by professional Fortnite players on Twitch identified recurring patterns and characteristics among profiles. In general, a very strong male presence was registered, with only one female player selected through the methodology presented, which favoured players with the highest number of wins in competitive tournaments on each continent. With regard to earnings, it is also noted that the African continent presents a disparity of values in relation to other continents. The highest prize value achieved by a player from Africa is below the lowest prize value achieved among selected profiles from all other continents.

With regard to the use of the platform, only two continents had players who, even though were best positioned with respect to tournament winnings, had no Twitch profiles. One of them is Africa, which does not have its own server for the game, which explains a smaller number of professional players dedicated to Fortnite. In Asia, other factors may be at stake. The continent has its own server, but in China, for example, which represents the largest market for esports and game streaming in the world (Newzoo Global Games Market Report, 2021), the title has been banned. In addition, there is also the possibility of using Twitch or competing platforms, such as AfreecaTV.

It was noticed, in all regions, that streamers do not have a fixed streaming schedule, with predefined times and dates. On the contrary, transmissions seem to happen spontaneously, with weeks in which there are several lives and weeks with only one or none.

In addition, on all continents, video content is often restricted to game matches. Only four profiles have shared anything beyond the gameplay itself. Two of them dealt only with Fortnite-related issues, such as Bugha, an American streamer who talks about aspects of the game and their reactions during some of the matches. Brothers Jesse and Jordan, from Oceania, have a profile together and sometimes close the game to open Twitter or YouTube and comment on leaks from the community or news to be released.

Among the profiles of African nationality, there were two players who published content totally unrelated to video games. The streamer Flyz streamed himself watching videos or fooling around with his friends. Pokimane, a Moroccan girl who grew up in Canada and currently lives in the United States, brought a greater diversity of content to her profile. In addition to playing different titles, she also broadcast "just chatting", a platform tag to indicate lives based on the conversation between streamer and audience. It is worth emphasizing that, despite having participated in competitive tournaments, the streamer is currently more focused on content creation and holds great popularity in the community, with almost 9 million followers.

In general, transmission time ranges from 1 to 2 hours to 11 hours uninterrupted. There are profiles that, in addition to full streams, also post videos of highlights with short excerpts normally posted by other users and indexed to their profile. This is the case of Aqua, from Austria, and Bugha, from the United States, for example. There are also profiles with no full streaming, only with short-indexed videos, such as Rojo from the Netherlands and Peterpan_fn, a Korean streamer, and the only Asian player included in the sample, who had content available on Twitch. In addition, there are profiles without any video, such as that of Canadian Zayt and Japanese RizArt.

The broadcasts show different degrees of professionalism. Eight profiles have investment from sponsors and show ads on their presentation page or in broadcast matches interface, as is done on television during sports matches. European streamer nicknamed Wolfiez even carried the sponsors' logo on their main page banner. Seven of the profiles do not have any brand sponsorship; they only disclosed their social media and links to donations or to the team's website. Seven of the profiles bore a description of the team the player belonged to, while eight of them were not linked to any team.

It is noted that four players did not have active Twitch profiles, and two of them had a channel together, totalling 15 active profiles. The variations between the use of the platform by streamers was more related to the objective of the channel and the level of investment than to the country or continent of origin. However, the fact that African streamers have less reach and structure than the others cannot be omitted, and those who are more professional do not currently reside in their countries of origin.

Webcam use seems to be a factor that generates interest and engagement during matches. When they use it, they insert their image into a frame next to the gameplay. In such cases, the streamer usually indicates in the title of the video that it is a broadcast with facecam. There was a peculiar case of player Volx, from Oceania, who indicated that some videos would include facecam, but left only his static image throughout the broadcast. This was done in more than one video, perhaps to attract more attention and community engagement, or as a joke with their viewers. Bugha, for example, in some transmissions showed his keyboard, mouse, and the movements he made while playing instead of showing his face on camera.

The way players deal with the audience on the platform varies, but in most cases a low interaction between streamers and audience has been identified during lives, regardless of the continent. There are broadcasts in which the player only chats with other players who are in the match with him, and cases where there is no conversation at all, with players just broadcasting their screen in silence. On the other hand, there are profiles that are more engaged in these relationships. European player Nythrox, for example, played with some of his Twitter followers and chatted with them via voice chat. He also has a wall on his profile that indicates a ranking of the most engaged users in his profile, through comments, subscriptions, or donations. The Volx profile, from Oceania, uses a command that allows fans who are commenting on the broadcast chat to appear in the interface of the gameplay itself.

On Twitter, in addition to standing as relevant sources within the Fortnite universe, disseminating first-hand information, and resonating the developments of the game, the profiles of players Kyle, Harrison, Shane, and Williams mobilize millions of interactors. This ability to engage and the relevance of players from the American continent in microblogging can be seen on the blue verification seal. Issued to all monitored accounts, the seal attests, based on the criteria of the social media itself, that the profile in question is authentic, viewable, and active. That is, the page includes microblogging conversations, presents a considerable rate of daily references and growth of followers, is referenced by large media companies, and reports official data related to the teams and organizations it integrates (Twitter, 2021).

By sharing their views on Fortnite releases, promoting promotional actions, colabs with other brands, and commenting on their performance in the competition, the tweets posted by players meet Twitter's always-on temporality. Although they produce little content, since most posts are RTs from other profiles, the tweets, mostly with few characters, reverberate the immediacy of events. The network conversation generated by American players provided only symmetrical connections, that is, it was limited only to interactors that followed each other. Thus, references and collaboration encouragement were limited to other professional players, teams, brands, and sponsors.

The main focus of content published by profiles is the Universe of Fortnite; the game guides individualization resources and communication exchanges. In this context, the pages feature elements such as avatar, cover, and username related to the game. As for communication layers, they are all guided by issues related to Fortnite, the indexations are those officially launched by the teams and/or by the game itself, the references are restricted to the scope of the universe, etc. In this sense, in order to understand the tweets shared by the pages, the interactor would have to be fully familiar with the game. Multimodal features used by players integrate the redirection of followers to other platforms (YouTube, Twitch, and specialized sites), images of rankings, and rounds scores videos with excerpts from matches and photos of everyday life. According to Winn and Heeter (2008) and Taylor (2011, 2018) in the video game environment, particularly esports, masculinity is staged mainly in competitive areas through the association between play and sport, not only reinforcing hypermasculinized behaviours, but also marginalizing, sexualizing, and excluding women. The day-to-day images of Kyle, Harrison, Shane, and Williams endorse, even indirectly, these performative effects of sexuality and gender. Whether through the sharing of photos and retweeting comments from follow-ers, who praise the body of their girlfriends and/or in selfies in front of the mirror highlighting muscles, the lifestyle exposed by players is guided by heteronormativity patterns.

The profiles of players on the European continent reflect informa-tion, ratings and, particularly, commercial releases related to Fortnite. The sale of products includes setup items, discounts skins and licensed packages, and clothes licensed by the teams. In addition to being led by the continuous present of microblogging, the publications perform a kind of curatorship of the main news on the Universe of Fortnite. Players share news broadcast by the specialized press and the fran-chise official website, centralizing and selecting the content that is most relevant to the franchise-consuming audience.

The asymmetric connections and collaboration between the mem-bers were observed punctually during the monitoring of the profiles of David, Emil, Jaden, and Dave. For example, the tweet posted by David, in which he asks his followers to share photos of their setups. Multimodal features have been used to redirect interactors to other platforms (YouTube, Twitch, and product sales sites), screenshots of Fortnite interface, gamers' lifestyle photos, and memes.

The images posted by David, Emil, Jaden, and Dave showed travel records, team training venues, the most listened to songs by players, and setups. Pictures of setups published during the monitoring period contrasted their current equipment with equipment used at the beginning of their careers. Despite leaving the Fortnite universe, memes made a correlation between the game and the football universe. Players such as Ronaldo and Messi were often used to bolster the tal-ent of the franchise's professional players and the fierce competition of matches.

The profiles of Ibrahima, Aitouadda, VoltiaX, and Imane, from the African continent, presented different ways of understanding the informational architecture and content production. In this context, the pages managed by players Ibrahima and VoltiaX do not present a communication strategy directed to Twitter. That is, in the monitoring period the published tweets replicated only information from other profiles. RTs cover only their respective teams, other professional players, and sponsors, as well as automatic sharing of platforms such as YouTube and Wiki. Thus, despite having a considerable average of tweets, except for a few one-off posts, pages function only as a space for the reproduction of outsourced information.

Aitouadda and Imane's profiles, on the other hand, present a strategy of engagement in dialogue with the specifics of Twitter. Tweets posted by players reflected the releases and events related to the Fortnite franchise, lives on Twitch, and day-to-day training of the team. The temporality of microblogging matches publications on other topics, not restricted to the Fortnite universe. Aitouadda, for example, comments on the broadcasts of French football matches and the performance on the pitch of MBappé, PSG.

Asymmetric connections can be observed on both pages; Aitouadda encourages the participation and formation of momentary communities by reporting their daily lives, asking followers about Nike's tennis models, highlighting the details of their setup, etc. Imane's profile conversations usually start with subjects that are not related to Fortnite; the player asks for series tips, shows her 'looks of the day', her skincare routine, approaching the communication model adopted by influencers.

Multimodal features integrate sharing of pictures, video, game interface screenshots with playability rating and information, redirection to other platforms (YouTube and Twitch), and memes. In this context, it is important to emphasize that the images published by the player Aitouadda objectify women; the tweets show models in sensual poses, reinforcing the performance effects of gender. Although directed to the audience that consumes Fortnite franchise, the content produced by Aitouadda and Imane can be understood by different interactors, not limited to familiarity with the universe of the plot. In this way, football, fashion, and music enthusiasts may be interested in the microblogging posts.

Players from the Asian continent Sung, Jong, Maufin, and RizArt reflected recent Fortnite developments, such as ranking, team performance, skins and packages offers, as well as details of their training routines. In this context, the temporality of Twitter allowed interactors to follow, in real time, updates of the preparation process of each player. Asymmetric connections were not observed during the monitoring period; in this sense profile interactions were limited to references to profiles of teams, sponsors, and other professional players of the franchise. Tweets published by Sung, Jong, Maufin, and RizArt reinforce the game universe through promotional images, interface screenshots, highlighting individual and respective team rankings, video excerpts of matches, links to other platforms (YouTube, Discord and sites selling specialized items), and everyday pictures. As observed on other pages, marketing of items is recurrent. On the other hand, day-to-day images shared on the pages highlight mainly material goods, such as the purchase of the first apartment or of a new car.

Published in two languages (English and Japanese), the content produced by Asian players caused repercussions on different audiences. In addition to posts related to the Fortnite universe, profiles also covered various areas of Japanese culture, such as anime, cooking, and Pokemon universe. The identity of Fortnite players was constantly enhanced in the individualization features of the pages and in the dissemination of skins used by players.

Monitoring for Oceania players covered the Twitter pages of Jesse, Jordan, Volx, and Abdullah. However, it is important to mention that brothers Jesse and Jordan share the same profile, @x2twins, and Volx posted only 13 tweets during the monitoring period, 12^2 of which were retweets from other pages. In this way, the analysis will focus on two pages: brothers Jesse and Jordan's and Abdullah's.

Twitter instantaneity is present in tweets that reflect lives made by players and real-time comments about matches. In this way, by accessing microblogging, interactors could follow the views of players on the developments of the game. Despite engaging the audience around launches and match results, generating high metrics, the profiles did not provide the formation of asymmetric connections. Multimodal features can be seen in posting pictures of players routine, sharing images of equipment, setup, selfies, etc., with followers, redirecting to other platforms (YouTube and Twitch), and the constant use of emojis.

Final considerations

Despite starting from different social, cultural, and technological contexts, the profiles of professional players analysed on Twitch and Twitter have some characteristics that should be highlighted.

In Twitch it was noticed that, even among those who have great reach and popularity within the community, only few hold a professional transmedia planning of profiles performance. There is a certain degree of amateurism in various aspects related to video and interaction with viewers – for instance, creation of channels' visual identity; composition of video titles, often random; irregularity in posts and broadcasts; and little interaction with fans during lives. On all continents, there have been cases of random images, such as cartoon prints or animal photos, used as a profile picture or banner. The lack of greater attention to broadcast or interaction with fans can be partly justified by the fact that most players analysed have profiles of pro players, i.e., professional players with a focus on performance and competitive tournaments, rather than content producers or influencers. However, there are profiles that also manage channels on YouTube and other social media and are more focused on the idea of generating regular content for their audience, such as Pokimane and brothers Jesse and Jordan, but it is still remarkable to notice the lack of mediation, support, or interest on the part of most streamers in making their profile more professional.

On Twitter, the content published by professional players communicates directly with the audience to which they are directed, providing access to information and repercussions on the releases, lives, and developments of Fortnite matches in real time, synchronously with broadcasts on Twitch and YouTube. In this context, the characteristic elements of each player, such as the skin, are reinforced in the individualization features and in screenshots (images and video) of the game. Although the characteristics of informational architecture, such as the focus of social interaction and the use of indexing in the segmentation of themes, are not in operation in tweets, the 'always on' temporality and multimodal features are points that guide the production of content in microblogging. Another relevant point to be highlighted is the role that Twitter plays in players' transmedia communication strategies. Although some pages establish actions directed to the social network, in general, publications are in dialogue, even indirectly, with content published on other platforms, such as Twitch and YouTube.

Thus, data produced in this research can give rise to other studies to deepen the insight on the use of other social media, such as YouTube and Instagram, in order to understand transmedia performance strategies of profiles studied in other networks.

Acknowledgements

Many thanks to Gustavo Furtuoso Ribeiro, undergraduate research fellow, who collaborated in the data collection of the research that originated this chapter.

This work is financed by national funds from Portugal through the FCT - Fundação para a Ciência e a Tecnologia, I.P., under the UIDB/04019/2020 and UIDP/04019/2020.

References

Blog Twitter. (2022, January 10). *2021: An exceptional year for Gaming on Twitter.* https://bit.ly/3AkaaSI

Burroughs, B., & Rama, P. (2015). The eSports Trojan Horse: Twitch and streaming futures. *Journal for Virtual Worlds Research, 8*(2), 1–5. https://doi.org/10.4101/jvwr.v8i2.7176

Devia-Allen, G. (2017). *Good game well played: an esports documentary* [Master's thesis, Illinois State University] ProQuest. https://ir.library.illinoisstate.edu/etd/663

Hamilton, W., Garretson, O., & Kerne, A. (2014). Streaming on twitch: fostering participatory communities of play within live mixed media. In *Proceedings of the SIGCHI Conference on Human Factors in Computing Systems* (CHI'14), (pp. 1315–1324). https://doi.org/10.1145/2556288.2557048

Help Center. (2021, December 23). *About verified accounts, Twitter.* https://bit.ly/3fRg30z

Hutchins, B. (2008). Signs of meta-change in second modernity: the growth of e-sport and the World Cyber Games. *New Media & Society, 10*(6), 851–869. https://doi.org/10.1177/1461444808096248

Jenson, J., & de Castell, S. (2018). "The entrepreneurial gamer": regendering the order of play. *Games and Culture, 13*(7), 728–746. https://doi.org/10.1177/1555412018755913

Kaytoue, M., Silva, A., Cerf, L., Meira, W., & Raïssi, C. (2012). Watch me playing, I am a professional: a first study on video game live streaming. In *WWW'12 Companion Proceedings of the 21st International Conference on World Wide Web* (pp. 1181–1188). https://doi.org/10.1145/2187980.2188259

Macedo, T., & Falcão, T. (2019). E-Sports, heirs to a tradition. *Intext, 45*(2), 246–267. https://doi.org/10.19132/1807-858320190.246-267

Márquez, F. V., & García, S. A. (2020). The video game Fortnite and the social network Twitter. In F.V Máquez & S. A García.(Eds.) *Management and audiovisual training to create content on social networks* (pp. 637–651). Madrid: McGraw-Hill Interamericana.

Newzoo Global Esports and Streaming Market Report. (2021). *Global Esports & live streaming market report.* https://bit.ly/3KETw59

Newzoo Global Games Market Report. (2021). *Global games market report the VR & Metaverse edition.* https://bit.ly/3GZL1PQ

Newzoo Trends to Watch Report. (2021). *Games, Esports, and mobile trends to watch in 2021.* https://bit.ly/3Arsn0V

Puertos Amat, A. (2021). *Analysis of the influence of Twitter on the interest and consumption of video games on Twitch* [Doctoral dissertation] Universitat Politècnica de València. RiuNet. https://riunet.upv.es/handle/10251/171301

Reitman, J. G., Anderson-Coto, M. J., Wu, M., Lee, J. S., & Steinkuehler, C. (2020). Esports research: a literature review. *Games and Culture, 15*(1), 32–50. https://doi.org/10.1177/1555412019840892

Steinkuehler, C. (2020). Esports research: critical, empirical, and historical studies of competitive videogame play. *Games and Culture, 15*(1), 3–8. https://doi.org/10.1177/1555412019836855

Taylor, N. (2011). Play globally, act locally: the standardization of Pro Halo 3 Gaming. *International Journal of Gender, Science and Technology, 3* (1), 1–15. https://bit.ly/3FJPJQn

Taylor, N. (2016a). Now you're playing with audience power: the work of watching games. *Critical Studies in Media Communication, 3*(4), 293–307. https://doi.org/10.1080/15295036.2016.1215481

Taylor, N. (2016b). Play to the camera: video ethnography, spectatorship, and e-sports. *Convergence, 22*(2), 115–130. https://doi.org/10.1177/1354856515580282

Taylor, N., Jenson, J., & de Castell, S. (2009). Cheerleaders/booth babes/ Halo hoes: pro-gaming, gender and jobs for the boys, *Digital Creativity, 20*(4), 239–252. https://doi.org/10.1080/14626260903290323

Taylor, N., & Voorhees, G. (Eds.). (2018). *Masculinities in play.* Carter County, OK: Springer.

Taylor, T. L. (2015). *Raising the stakes: Esports and the professionalization of computer gaming.* Cambridge, MA: MIT Press.

Winn, J.; Heeter, C. (2009). Gaming, gender, and time: Who makes time to play?. *Sex Roles, 61*(1–2), 1–13. https://doi.org/10.1007/s11199-009-9595-7

Witkowski, E. (2012). On the digital playing field how we "do sport" with networked computer games. *Games and Culture, 7*(5), 349–374. https://doi.org/10.1177/1555412012454222

Wohn, D. Y., & Freeman, G. (2020). Live streaming, playing, and money spending behaviors in eSports. *Games and Culture, 15*(1), 73–88. https://doi.org/10.1177/1555412019859184

Wulf, T., Schneider, F. M., & Beckert, S. (2020). Watching players: an exploration of media enjoyment on twitch. *Games and Culture, 15*(3), 328–346. https://doi.org/10.1177/1555412018788161

Notes

1 Available at: https://www.esportsearnings.com/. Accessed: 18 January 2022.
2 The only tweet posted by the player is "hey guys".

6 How the Negative Public View of Videogames Threatens Esports Sponsors

Bruno Duarte Abreu Freitas and
Ruth S. Contreras-Espinosa

Introduction

Esports – short for electronic sports – are closely connected to the now antiquated LAN parties where gamers would gather, in a real-world location, to compete in relatively small-scale and friendly videogame matches (Shabir, 2017). With the appearance of easily accessible high-speed internet and streaming functionalities, however, this changed (Carter & Gibbs, 2013) and gave birth to the modern, serious, and large-scale esports competitions that have been popularized around the globe (Ströh, 2017). In this sense, the current esports can be understood as professionally orchestrated videogame tournaments where the best players in the world – commonly dubbed pro-gamers or pro-players – participate (Shabir, 2017) to acquire prestige, money, and prizes (Mooney, 2018). It must be kept in mind that esports is a collective term, meaning that, like water sports, they are composed of different activities, which in this case are competitions around different videogames (Ströh, 2017). Furthermore, there are different tournament tiers (Shabir, 2017), like semi-amateur and professional (SuperData, 2017a). While low-tier tournaments generally occur with pro-gamers competing from home via internet connections (Stein & Scholz, 2016), the majority of high-tier tournaments require pro-gamers to gather in a specific real-world location – like a stadium – to compete, and fans watch either in person or online (Gifford, 2017).

The recent advancements in internet speed and streaming technologies mean that esports were only able to reach high levels of popularity recently in the early 2010s (Ströh, 2017). Nevertheless, in just a few years, they rapidly grew (Shabir, 2017) to become a worldwide recognized phenomenon. Several countries, like South Korea, now recognize competitive gaming as a sport (Hiltscher & Scholz, 2017). Moreover, they are not only the world's fastest-growing sport (Sylvester &

DOI: 10.4324/9781003273691-9

Rennie, 2017), but also one of the fastest-growing industries overall (Winnan, 2016). Their high popularity (CGC Europe, 2015), large worldwide reach (BI Intelligence & Elder, 2017), and relevant economic strength (Shabir, 2017) is attracting numerous consumer brands looking to use them as a marketing channel (CGC Europe, 2015). For instance, brands signed over 600 esports sponsorship contracts in just 2016 (Shabir, 2017). Some notable brands include Vodafone, Coca-Cola (Ströh, 2017), Audi, Google, Nissan, Paris Saint-German, Sony, Manchester City (Shabir, 2017), Samsung, Microsoft, and Red Bull (Funk, Pizzo, & Baker, 2018).

The popularity around competitive gaming is leading sponsors to gain some major return on investments (ROIs) (Freitas et al., 2020), particularly a significant boost in brand awareness (Ströh, 2017). This is because, in 2020, there were already 495 million esports fans (Newzoo, 2020a; Statista, 2020), a figure that has been enjoying a yearly increase of between 10.4% and 12.3% (Newzoo, 2020a). Ergo, some studies predict that, in 2023, there will be roughly 646 million esports fans (Newzoo, 2020a; Statista, 2020), a number that is larger than the NFL's entire fan base and in line with the fandom of various other popular sports (Shabir, 2017). The popularity of esports is so large that it already receives higher viewership numbers when compared to several well-known sports (Winnan, 2016). For instance, although the 2014 match between USA and Germany in the Football World Championship had a respectable 1.7 million viewers on ESPN (CGC Europe, 2015), the esports tournament Katowice Intel Extreme Masters had an outstanding 46 million viewers on YouTube and Twitch (Statista, 2018). Besides high exposure, competitive gaming sponsors are also enjoying increased sales figures (Freitas et al., 2020; Winnan, 2016). This is because the general esports fan, besides having an income that is above average (Ströh, 2017), is also a compulsive buyer, an early adopter of technology-related products (Winnan, 2016), and, most importantly, a strong influencer of his or her friends' and family's buying behavior (Ströh, 2017). Because of this, it was calculated that, in 2020, competitive gaming had a value of 1.34 billion US dollars (Pannekeet, 2019), a figure that is expected to have an annual growth of 9.7% (SuperData, 2017b). Furthermore, contrary to the majority of established sports, whose survivability is not entirely dependent on sponsor funds, the competitive gaming market, which is still in its early stages, is largely dependent on sponsor money to survive (Ströh, 2017). Because esports are unable to exist, in their current large scale, without sponsors, it is much cheaper to sponsor them than regular sports (Winnan, 2016).

As is evident, competitive gaming is a novel and exciting market whose benefits are attracting several sponsors (Freitas et al., 2020). However, despite this high popularity, the esports industry is still susceptible to some threats (Mooney, 2018; Shabir, 2017; Ströh, 2017; Winnan, 2016) that carry the potential of seriously damaging its entire market (Shabir, 2017; Ströh, 2017; Winnan, 2016). Hence, it is imperative that esports sponsors become aware of the risks that come with sponsoring competitive gaming because these can negatively affect their brands in multiple ways (Ströh, 2017).

Although gaming is extremely popular nowadays (Newman, 2008; Shabir, 2017; Ströh, 2017; Winnan, 2016), it still has a negative image in society (AEVI, 2018; Franke, 2015; Hilvoorde, 2016; Peša et al., 2017). Unlike, sports, videogames are, in general, still not accepted by society (Peša et al., 2017). This stigma is, in fact, quite notorious (Li, 2016; Shabir, 2017), and this is a challenge to brands because there is a chance that the negativity around gaming may spread to the esports sponsors, damaging them (Ströh, 2017). Some of the critiques videogames receive include the damaging of productivity, creativity, and literacy (Newman, 2008), as well as lowering school grades, encouraging sedentary behavior, promoting obesity, and destroying reading habits (Tavinor, 2009). The act of playing a videogame is essentially seen as an unproductive activity where the gamer behaves like a mindless sheep that is completely absorbed by the game's virtual world and stimuli. This unfavorable view has led a multitude of people to infer that gamers should make better use of their time by performing more energetic and enriching activities (Newman, 2008).

Since the act of playing a videogame is perceived as an activity where the gamer is detached from the real world (Li, 2016), it is usually understood as an antisocial act (Brookey & Oates, 2015; Newman, 2008) that may promote social isolation (Peša et al., 2017). Likewise, playing a videogame is believed to be an unhealthy act (Brookey & Oates, 2015), which creates the perception that gamers are sick people who spend eight hours per day mindlessly staring at screens (Shabir, 2017). Subsequently, esports are now observed as a danger to people's health due to the dangerous fusion of inactivity and participants of a very young age demographic (Holden et al., 2018).

Competitive gaming is also famously seen as belonging to a nerd culture (Taylor, 2012). Even today, it is almost impossible to escape the derogatory portrayal of gamers as being overweight nerds who eat too many Cheetos and drink Mountain Dew and live in their parents' basements (Li, 2016). Furthermore, unfortunately, there is the stigma that gamers pay more attention to videogames than to their jobs. These negative views are so persistent and strong that, when an employer analyzes a person's curriculum vitae, the employer will usually favor someone who did voluntary work in a sporting club over someone who has several years of experience as an administrator of a popular esports enterprise (Scholz, 2010b).

The inciting of violence has also become another negative stereotype (Hilvoorde, 2016; Scholz, 2010a; Ströh, 2017), along with gaming leading to truancy, theft, and drug use (Shabir, 2017). This has led gamers to be seen as friendless and maladjusted loners who favor the comfort of the virtual world over being with real people. And this, in turn, has created the myth that gamers are obsessive, unbalanced, and dangerous. Ergo, all events connected with violence or aggression (particularly school shootings) are commonly inferred to have been promoted by exposure to videogames (Newman, 2008). Likewise, the competitive gaming market is susceptible to the negative portrayal of violent videogames by the media. This adverse publicity puts esports under pressure because it may lead current, and potential, industry partners to leave. Brands may wish to terminate their esports sponsorships to prevent suffering collateral damage if, for instance, the mass media blames videogames for another school shooting incident (Ströh, 2017).

Gaming has also been blamed for being addictive (Ackerman, 2016; Tavinor, 2009), and the truth is that some studies have found very convincing evidence that gaming addiction may happen when people play videogames for long periods of time (Shabir, 2017). Even so, the strong competition among esports players requires them to have this taxing lifestyle if they want to be a top player (Stivers, 2017). Just like with any other profession, pro-gamers are professionals who understand that their salaries are at stake (Parkin, 2015), so it is common for the best pro-players to play videogames for 16 hours per day (Taylor, 2012). In this regard, competitive gaming is just like regular sports. If one wishes to be the best, sacrifices must be made (Parkin, 2015). Still, this grueling work ethic has caused the hospitalization of some pro-players (Stivers, 2017; Wilson, 2017) and the death of others (Şentuna & Kanbur, 2016). Furthermore, there are several negative psychological effects that can be caused by excessive gaming (Şentuna & Kanbur, 2016), like depression, ADHD, anxiety, and the famous Tetris Effect (Holden et al., 2018).

Interestingly, gambling addiction can also be caused by exposure to esports (Macey & Hamari, 2018; Teichert et al., 2017). Several people are developing adverse gambling behaviors due to how easy it is to wager on videogame skins in gambling websites (Teichert et al., 2017).

And the more they watch competitive gaming, the more probable it is that they will develop addictions related to esports gambling (Macey & Hamari, 2018). The seriousness of this issue is catapulted by the young age of most esports fans (Gainsbury et al., 2017a, 2017b) because they are more prone to developing gambling addiction issues than older individuals (Gainsbury et al., 2017b). Moreover, the esports wagering industry has become so popular that it is already larger than the entire esports economy (Gainsbury et al., 2017a), and is now the seventh most popular wagering market (Winnan, 2016).

Every single one of these elements has a negative influence on how society perceives individuals whose career is centered around video-games (AEVI, 2018). Regrettably, it is difficult to erase from society's mind the image of the shut-in and antisocial gamer who is obsessed with videogames and convert it into the image of a smart, tech-savvy, and healthy individual (Liboriussen & Martin, 2016). This cloud of negativity over gaming presents, and will continue to present, severe risks to the promotion of competitive gaming (Taylor, 2012). Based on this data, we posit the following:

H_1:   The negative public view on videogames (which may come from the virtual violence or from gaming or gambling addiction) is a risk to esports sponsors.

Methodology

This study employed an exploratory design and a mixed method approach. The time horizon was cross-sectional, the study setting was non-contrived, and an overt stance was adopted by the researchers.

A sample of 5,638 esports fans was used. These individuals were selected through a nonprobability purposive heterogeneous sampling method. Particularly, there was a purposeful selection of a diverse group of fans to ensure that the sample included as many unique fan perspectives as possible. To reach this diverse sample, a database was created and it comprised the 103 most popular esports games – at the time of the data collection. This database served as a guide to select the most relevant esports-related communities on Discord and Reddit – called Discord Channels and subreddits, respectively. Here we selected subreddits and Discord Channels related to one or more of the 103 games of the database. The focus was on Discord and Reddit because, according to Lee (2017), these are the two most used social websites by the videogame community. To create the database, the data from Newzoo (2020b) – which shows the 20 most viewed esports games from January to May 2019 – was combined with the data from Esports Earnings (2020) – which shows the 100 esports games that have awarded the total highest prize money. Esports and Newzoo are commonly used by multiple researchers, like Owens (2016), Ströh (2017), Menasce (2019), Cunningham et al. (2018), Sylvester and Rennie (2017), Shabir (2017), and Jenny et al. (2018). Table 6.1 shows the aforesaid database.

Table 6.1 Most viewed and most prize money awarded to esports games

Esports videogames

Tekken 7	*PlayerUnknown's Battlegrounds*
Age of Empires II	*Mobile*
Call of Duty: Infinite Warfare	*Halo 5: Guardians*
Call of Duty: Modern Warfare 3	*Arena of Valor*
World of Tanks	*Shadowverse*
Blade & Soul	*Gwent*
World of WarCraft	*Paladins*
Clash of Clans	*Free Fire*
Call of Duty: Black Ops 2	*Guild Wars 2*
Hearthstone	*Super Smash Bros. Melee*
Team Fortress 2	*Dota 2*
KartRider	*Quake Champions*
FIFA Online 3	*rFactor 2*
Ultra Street Fighter IV	*Gears of War 4*
Brawlhalla	*Halo 2 Anniversary*
SMITE	*Injustice 2*
CrossFire	*FIFA 18*
Pro Evolution Soccer 2017	*F1 2019*
Super Smash Bros. Ultimate	*FIFA 17*
iRacing.com	*Pokémon: Let's Go, Pikachu! and*
Madden NFL 2018	*Eevee!*
Halo: Reach	*StarCraft II*
Halo: Combat Evolved	*Dead or Alive 4*
Old School Runescape	*Quake III Arena*
Fortnite	*Call of Duty: Black Ops III*
FIFA 19	*Project Gotham Racing 3*
Turbo Racing League	*Clash Royale*
Magic: The Gathering Arena	*Madden NFL 2017*
Defense of the Ancients	*Super Street Fighter IV Arcade*
StarCraft: Brood War	*Edition*
Counter-Strike: Global Offensive	*Rocket League*
World in Conflict	*Forza Motorsport 7*
Counter-Strike Online	*Vainglory*
Madden NFL 2013	*Street Fighter V*
Mortal Kombat 11	*Call of Duty: Ghosts*

Pokémon Sword/Shield	*FIFA 20*
Tom Clancy's Rainbow Six: Siege	*Call of Duty 4: Modern Warfare*
Mortal Kombat X	*Attack on Titan Tribute Game*
Magic: The Gathering Online	*League of Legends*
WarCraft III	*PlayerUnknown's Battlegrounds*
Counter-Strike	*Super Smash Bros. for Wii U*
Call of Duty: Black Ops 4	*TEPPEN*
Quake Live	*Apex Legends*
Quake 4	*Halo 3*
Halo 4	*NBA 2K18*
Street Fighter V: Arcade Edition	*Call of Duty: Advanced Warfare*
Call of Duty: Modern Warfare	*Call of Duty: Black Ops*
Point Blank	*Overwatch*
Call of Duty: World War II	*Halo 2*
Heroes of Newerth	*H1Z1*
FIFA 13	*Painkiller*
Teamfight Tactics	*Counter-Strike: Source*
	Auto Chess
	Heroes of the Storm

Note: Table based on the lists from Esports Earnings (2020) and Newzoo (2020b)

Since most esports fans have a high online affinity, a mostly closed-ended structured online questionnaire was used to collect the sample's data via self-recruitment and self-administration. Google Forms was used to develop this questionnaire, which is a popular online survey website suggested by various authors, including Cohen, Manion, and Morrison (2018). In total, the requests and link to fill out the questionnaire on Google Forms were posted in 263 Discord Channels and in 392 subreddits. To ensure that only esports fans participated in the research, the first question of the survey was a simple yes/no filter item asking "Do you regularly watch and/or participate in esports?" and those who selected "No" were not able to fill out the remainder of the questionnaire. This survey was pretested on 167 esports fans in esports-related subreddits and Discord Channels from 14 April 2019 to 25 May 2019. As for the real empirical data collection, it was between 29 June 2019 and 3 December 2019. The unit of observation was the individual, and the unit of analysis was the organization. The demographic data from the sample can be viewed in Table 6.2.

It was observed that the demographic characteristics of the study's sample are representative of the general esports population since they are largely in line with the data from the literature. Specifically, 92.7% of the sample comprised males, which is extremely close to

Table 6.2 Esports fans' demographics

	Valid	No answer	Valid (%)	Mean	SD	Mode
Age	5,412	226		23.05	6.062	18
Gender	5,560	78				
Female	407		7.3			
Male	5,153		92.7			
Ethnicity	5,477	161				
American Indian or Alaska Native	71		1.3			
Asian	824		15			
Black or African American	147		2.7			
Hispanic, Latino or Spanish origin	421		7.7			
Middle Eastern or North African	116		2.1			
Native Hawaiian or other Pacific Islander	38		.7			
White	4,255		77.7			
Other	197		3.6			
Region	5,553	85				
Africa	32		.6			
Asia	322		5.8			
Europe	1,860		33.5			
North America	3,013		54.3			
Oceania	191		3.4			
South America	135		2.4			
Education	5,497	141				
6th grade or less	11		.2			
7th to 12th grade	2,178		39.6			
Bachelor degree	2,332		42.4			
Master degree	525		9.6			
PhD	90		1.6			
Post-doctorate	16		.3			
Other	345		6.3			
Employment status	5,527	111				
Student	2,720		49.2			
Employed	2,293		41.5			
Homemaker	40		.7			
Unemployed	324		5.9			

Retired	17		.3
Other	133		2.4
Marital status	5,510	128	
Single	4,056		73.6
Cohabiting	932		16.9
Married	480		8.7
Divorced	33		.6
Widowed	9		.2

Note: N = sample size, SD = standard deviation. For ethnicity, participants were able to select more than one option

the data from Billings, Rodgers, Rodgers, and Wiggins (2019), who indicate that 92.4% of them are male and it is also close to the data from Zolides (2015), who points out that 90% of them are male. The average age of the sample was 23.05, which is in line with the 18- to 25-years-old presented by Mooney (2018) and is close to the average age of 26 pointed out by Nielsen Esports (2017). Unfortunately, it was not possible to compare the remainder of the sample's demographic data because it is not thoroughly covered in the literature and academia.

Because of the minute literature and academic attention on the topic of esports sponsorships, the questionnaire of this research had as few questions as possible so that the small questionnaire would attract as many participants as possible and thus catapult the relevance and significance of the results. Quantitative data were analyzed with IBM SPSS Statistics 25 and qualitative data with NVivo 10. In order to abide by the social norms of anonymity, the participants were not asked for any personal data (e.g. name, email address, phone number).

Results

Figure 6.1 shows the frequencies of the data obtained by asking the question "Do you think society still has a negative perception of videogames?" The answer options to this closed-ended question were "No", "Yes, some people have negative views on videogames", and "Yes, most people have negative views on videogames". Overall, it is possible to observe that 95.7% (i.e. n = 5,394/5,638) of the sample feels that people have, to some extent, negative views on gaming, and that 4.3% (i.e. n = 244/5,638) believe that people do not have this adverse perception.

Figure 6.2 shows the frequencies of the data obtained by asking the question "Has society's negative view on videogames ever led you to hide your interest for esports?" The answer options to this closed-ended question were "No", "Yes, sometimes", and "Yes, always". This item was contingent to the filter question "Do you think society still has a negative perception of videogames?" Particularly, only the fans that selected "Yes, some people have negative views on videogames" or "Yes, most people have negative views on videogames" were eligible to answer it. Overall, it is possible to observe that 56.2% (i.e. n = 3,031/5,394) of the sample had to hide

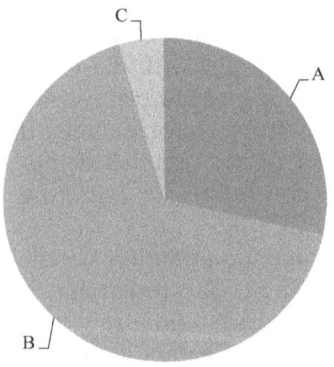

A. Yes, most people have negative views on videogames (28.7%; n = 1,615)

B. Yes, some people have negative views on videogames (67%; n = 3,779)

C. No, people do not have negative views on videogames (4.3%; n = 244)

Note. N = 5,638; n = 5,638; No answer = 0

Figure 6.1 Society's perception of videogames

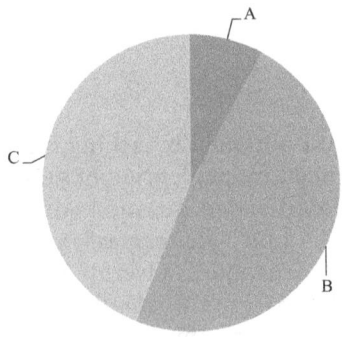

A. Yes, society's negative view on videogames has always led me to hide my interest for esports (8.1%; n = 438)

B. Yes, society's negative view on videogames has sometimes led me to hide my interest for esports (48.1%; n = 2,593)

C. No, society's negative view on videogames has never led me to hide my interest for esports (43.8%; n = 2,363)

Note. N = 5,638; n = 5,394; No answer = 244

Figure 6.2 Society's pressure to hide interest for competitive gaming

Table 6.3 Reasons that promote society's negative view on videogames

Subtheme and quote	Fan ID
Lack of acceptance of videogames and the need to better inform people	
"Video games are the future of entertainemtn and a huge money maker for sponsors and needs to be accepted asap".	16
"The biggest thing that esports should be striving towards is gaming and esports acceptance. It's still a huge problem for gaming that we just don't have the image that is beneficial. If we could show people that everyone can be a gamer then esports will blossom into something beautiful".	44
"Sponsors should be able to not only support a team, tournament, or organization, but also help increase viewership by marketing awareness of the game or team they sponsor outside of esports events, so that it (esports) loses the general stigma it has in the public's eye".	68
"Also possible avenue to better mainstream understanding/acceptance".	69
"Sponsor and esport cooperation is necessary for the growth and wide spread acceptance of esports".	75
"People should accept esports and video games more".	102
"One problem that the e-sports community faces is the lack of acceptance of video games. People who aren't interested in video games often look down 'gamers', and believe in the stereotype of unintelligent, angry, sweaty, unsocial, ultra nerdy, lazy, overweight, and misogynistic. If the public is shown how video games aren't these evil things, and a majority of 'gamers' don't match the stereotype, and acceptance of them is promoted it will entice more sponsors and help bring in more fans, even if they don't play, like how a majority of sports fans don't actually play the sport".	108
"Once people are more accepting of esports, they will try it".	173
"I think it's sad that despite the tremendous amount of work this industry can demand, and despite how exclusive it can be for people who aren't skillful players, people who participate in it don't always get a fair shake as would anyone with any other 9-5 job".	186
"Sponsors should not be the main way to get acceptance from society".	190
"I would like more sponsorships for non-meta games (like *fifa* mobile) and acceptance of e-gamer as a profession".	200
"Especially creating a positive view from society to esports".	203

(Continued)

Subtheme and quote	Fan ID
"As is, it's going to be extremely hard to get the average person to accept esports as a valid career choice".	208
"I think that once esports is widely accepted like other sports more sponsors will buy into esports".	216
"I love esports but I get mocked for doing what I love".	244
"I generally would like to see more acceptance in the public eye for especially from the older generation".	259
"If the sponsors are there only for the money, it doesnt really help esports that much in terms of popularity and acceptance".	292
"Also promoting video games as a sport and hobby from these sponsors would be important. Change the views of the public when it comes to video games".	293
"Esports is never going to catch on with older generations".	407
"ESports and video games not being considered a real sport or a joke and being laughed about is one of the main problems I often face/see. They aren't treated in the same way as physical sports".	410
Gaming addiction	
"We also need to make sure that people are educated on how to use gaming and e-sports effectively, to better their lives, rather than let them destroy themselves with addiction and the like".	14
"I really think videogames and especially E-sports have a bad influence on youth, with the dazzling prize money and huge sponsoring, it gives children the illusion that with enough practice you could be a pro, and a lot of kids fall into that trap and waste their time, forgetting it's only a game after all".	113
Virtual violence	
"Studies have shown that video games do not equal aggressiveness and irritablenes on a large enough scale to be concerning and a lot of schools are scared to add games like that for fear of being sued I feel like".	294
"In the US/society it's 'video games make school shooters' garbage. I think that if brands took more initiative to do stories on players and the games themselves it would make them more relatable and people would see it's not all the stereotypes of 'skinny white male with no friends school shooter' or 'fat neckbeard dude in his 30s living in their moms basement'".	312

their interest for competitive gaming to some extent, and that 43.8% (i.e. n = 2,363/5,394) never felt pressured to hide this interest.

The last question of the questionnaire was an open-ended and optional item asking "Would you like to add anything else about what was addressed in this survey?" Here, 24 fans provided answers connected to the topic of study. Table 6.3 shows the complete or partial quotes from these individuals. The quotes are arranged by reasons that promote society's negative view on videogames.

Discussion

The data confirmed H_1 that the negative public view on videogames is a threat to the sponsors of esports. According to the sample, most fans (i.e. 67%; n = 3,779/5,638) feel that some people possess negative views on videogames and a smaller, but still significant group (i.e. 28.7%; n = 1,615/5,638) believes that most individuals have these negative perspectives. Ergo, this implies that almost every single fan (i.e. 95.7%; n = 5,394/5,638) feels that society has negative views on videogames and just a very small number of fans (i.e. 4.3%; n = 244/5,638) does not feel that society possesses these adverse opinions. Going into greater detail, from the subsample that feels that people have negative views on videogames (i.e. 95.7%; n = 5,394/5,638), over half (i.e. 56.2%; n = 3,031/5,394) have felt pressured to conceal, to some extent, their interest for competitive gaming from society. Particularly, over half (i.e. 48.1%; n = 2,593/5,394) have, at least sometimes, had to hide their interest and a small number (i.e. 8.1%; n = 438/5,394) feel that they have been forced to always hide their interest for esports. Nevertheless, almost half of this subsample (i.e. 43.8%; n = 2,363/5,394) have never felt pressured to hide their interest for esports from society.

Overall, almost every esports fan feels that society has, to a certain degree, adverse perceptions on videogames and that, from these, over half have felt pressured to hide this interest for competitive gaming. Also, the sample's open-ended answers showed that fans feel that society wrongly believes that videogames promote aggressiveness. Likewise, fans largely commented on how society has a high lack of acceptance of gaming and that efforts should go into better educating them to not believe in the unfounded and adverse rumors that have continuously haunted the videogame industry and that, instead, they should be educated on the benefits of gaming. This was the most common argument. Still, fans agreed that esports and gaming can, in fact, cause addiction and that, to avoid this, effective preventive measured should be applied.

The empirical data was largely in line with the literature. The sample's data was in sync with Taylor (2012), Tavinor (2009), Shabir (2017), Peša et al. (2017), Newman (2008), Li (2016), Hilvoorde (2016), Franke (2015), Brookey and Oates (2015), and AEVI (2018), who point out that society usually has a negative perception of videogames, and with Peša et al. (2017), who indicates that videogames are not well accepted by some people. Multiple fans, as well as Ströh (2017), Shabir (2017), Scholz (2010a), Newman (2008), and Hilvoorde (2016), stated that society usually believes that gaming promotes real-world violence.

Interestingly, although Tavinor (2009), Shabir (2017), Scholz (2010b), Newman (2008), and Ackerman (2016) point out that society wrongly believes that gaming promotes addiction, Fan ID 14 and 113 commented that they feel that videogames can be addictive to some individuals and that suitable preventive measures should be applied. These comments are in sync with Shabir (2017), who states that multiple studies have shown that excessive gaming can lead to addiction.

Fan ID 108 as well as Peša et al. (2017), Newman (2008), Liboriussen and Martin (2016), and Brookey and Oates (2015) mentioned that society thinks that gaming promotes antisocial behaviors and isolation. Fan ID 108 also commented that society sees gamers as nerds, and this is in sync with the data from Taylor (2012) and Li (2016). Lastly, AEVI (2018) as well as Fan ID 186, 200, 208, 244, and 410 mentioned that society does not take seriously people who turn gaming into a career.

Conclusions

The overall findings carry significant and highly relevant implications for all current, and potential, esports sponsors that wish to obtain a better understanding of how the negative public view on gaming can negatively affect their brands. As Newman (2008) indicates, since its creation, society has negatively perceived gaming. Therefore, it is only logical for consumer brands to be hesitant to connect their companies with esports and this research showed that this hesitation is justified.

There is the ever-present risk of the sponsoring brand being damaged by a negative brand image transfer, and this threat becomes even greater if the brand is sponsoring violent videogames or if there have been any real-world acts of violence. If, in the recent years, there have been real-world acts of violence in the country where the esports tournament is taking place, then the danger of the sponsor's image being negatively affected catapults. Esports sponsors should be especially watchful of this latter detail. Also, despite multiple scientific articles showing that videogames do not promote aggressive behaviors, and although the most serious or large-scale incidents of violence across the world are not linked to gaming, the companies that sponsor violent videogames can still suffer from collateral damage and have their brand image damaged. Because of this, companies that sponsor non-violent videogames are much less prone to suffer from this threat. Nevertheless, it is better for brands to not publicly criticize violent videogames because this may lead esports fans to develop a negative perception of the company.

This does not mean that companies that just focus on the sponsoring of non-violent games are protected from being negatively perceived by society. The stigma around gaming is so pervasive that just being associated with any kind of videogame can be detrimental. Thus, it is suggested that brands base their decision to sponsor esports on two elements. First, brands should bear in mind their target audience. If the brand is endemic to esports and gaming, then it will not be much affected by this threat because their only consumers are gaming and esports fans, not the general public who has a negative opinion on videogames. Even if society in general becomes aware that this brand is sponsoring esports, and develops a negative perception of the company, the brand will not be affected because these individuals would never buy any of the company's products despite it sponsoring esports or not. In terms of non-endemic companies (i.e. those that target both gaming fans and the general public), a careful consideration should go into determining if esports fans constitute an audience attractive enough to justify taking this risk and if the countries where their most lucrative target audiences reside tend to have adverse perceptions of gaming. Second, brands should bear in mind their partners, investors, and shareholders. If the company's business connections value modernity, as well as current and up-to-date trends, the sponsoring competitive gaming is prone to catapult how positively these business partners perceive the brand. However, if the company's business connections do not value any of these elements, much less gaming, then it may be better to not associate with esports.

Despite the risks, and just like multiple authors and fans mentioned, esports and gaming in general are starting to become more accepted by society. It is true that, at this time, companies that sponsor competitive gaming are likely to be, to some extent, negatively perceived for associating themselves with videogames, but the seriousness of the dangers that accompany this threat are steadily decreasing.

References

Ackerman, D. (2016). *The Tetris effect: the game that hypnotized the world.* New York: PublicAffairs.

AEVI. (2018). *Libro blanco de los esports en España.* Retrieved from http://www. aevi.org.es/web/wp-content/uploads/2018/05/ES_libroblanco_online.pdf

BI Intelligence, & Elder, R. (2017, March 15). The eSports competitive video gaming market continues to grow revenues & attract investors. *Business Insider.* Retrieved 22 February, 2018, from http://www.businessinsider. com/esports-market-growth-ready-for-mainstream-2017-3

Billings, A. C., Rodgers, E. B. D., Rodgers, R. P., & Wiggins, B. P. (2019). Esports spectator motivation. In R. Rogers (Ed.), *Understanding Esports: an introduction to the global phenomenon* (pp. 73–84). London: Rowman & Littlefield.

Brookey, R. A., & Oates, T. P. (Eds.). (2015). *Playing to win.* Bloomington: Indiana University Press.

Carter, M., & Gibbs, M. (2013). eSports in EVE online: skullduggery, fair play and acceptability in an unbounded competition. In G. N. Yannakakis, E. Aarseth, K. Jørgensen, & J. C. Lester (Eds.), *Proceedings of the 8th International Conference on the Foundations of Digital Games* (pp. 47–54). Chania: Society for the Advancement of the Science of Digital Games.

CGC Europe. (2015). Marketing channel eSports – how to get the attention of young adults? Retrieved 19 January, 2018, from http://docplayer.net/ 12867287-Marketing-channel-esports-how-to-get-the-attention-of-young-adults.html

Cohen, L., Manion, L., & Morrison, K. (2018). *Research methods in education* (8th ed.). Abingdon: Routledge.

Cunningham, G. B., Fairley, S., Ferkins, L., Kerwin, S., Lock, D., Shaw, S., & Wicker, P. (2018). eSport: construct specifications and implications for sport management. *Sport Management Review, 21*(1), 1–6. https://doi.org/ 10.1016/j.smr.2017.11.002

Esports Earnings. (2020). Top games awarding prize money. Retrieved 28 January, 2020, from https://www.esportsearnings.com/games

Franke, T. (2015). The perception of eSports – mainstream culture, real sport and marketisation. In J. Hiltscher & T. M. Scholz (Eds.), *eSports yearbook 2013/14* (pp. 111–144). Norderstedt: Books on Demand GmbH. Retrieved from http://esportsyearbook.com/eyb201314.pdf

Freitas, B. D. A., Contreras-Espinosa, R. S., & Correia, P. Á. P. (2020). Identifying the pros, cons and tactics of eSports sponsorships: an integrative literature review. *Comunicação Pública, 15*(28). https://doi.org/10.4000/ cp.7243

Funk, D. C., Pizzo, A. D., & Baker, B. J. (2018). eSport management: embracing eSport education and research opportunities. *Sport Management Review, 21*(1), 7–13. https://doi.org/10.1016/j.smr.2017.07.008

Gainsbury, S. M., Abarbanel, B., & Blaszczynski, A. (2017a). Game on: comparison of demographic profiles, consumption behaviors, and gambling site selection criteria of esports and sports bettors. *Gaming Law Review, 21*(8), 575–587. https://doi.org/10.1089/glr2.2017.21813

Gainsbury, S. M., Abarbanel, B., & Blaszczynski, A. (2017b). Intensity and gambling harms: exploring breadth of gambling involvement among esports bettors. *Gaming Law Review, 21*(8), 610–615. https://doi.org/10.1089/glr2.2017.21812

Gifford, C. (2017). *Gaming record breakers.* London: Carlton Books Limited.

Hiltscher, J., & Scholz, T. M. (2017). Preface. In J. Hiltscher & T. M. Scholz (Eds.), *esports yearbook 2015/16* (pp. 7–8). Norderstedt: Books on Demand GmbH. Retrieved from http://www.esportsyearbook.com/eyb201516.pdf

Hilvoorde, I. V. (2016). Sport and play in a digital world. *Sport, Ethics and Philosophy, 10*(1), 1–4. https://doi.org/10.1080/17511321.2016.1171252

Holden, J. T., Kaburakis, A., & Rodenberg, R. M. (2018). Esports: children, stimulants and video-gaming-induced inactivity. *Journal of Paediatrics and Child Health.* https://doi.org/10.1111/jpc.13897

Jenny, S. E., Keiper, M. C., Taylor, B. J., Williams, D. P., Gawrysiak, J., Manning, R. D., & Tutka, P. M. (2018). eSports venues: a new sport business opportunity. *Journal of Applied Sport Management, 10*(1), 34–49. https://doi.org/10.18666/JASM-2018-V10-I1-8469

Lee, J. (2017, November 27). 3 awesome social networks just for gamers. Retrieved 19 October, 2019, from https://www.makeuseof.com/tag/3-awesome-social-networks-just-for-gamers/

Li, R. (2016). *Good luck have fun: the rise of eSports.* New York: Skyhorse Publishing.

Liboriussen, B., & Martin, P. (2016). Special issue: games and gaming in China. *Games and Culture, 11*(3), 227–232. https://doi.org/10.1177/1555412015615296

Macey, J., & Hamari, J. (2018). Investigating relationships between video gaming, spectating esports, and gambling. *Computers in Human Behavior, 80*, 344–353. https://doi.org/10.1016/j.chb.2017.11.027

Menasce, R. M. (2019). From casual to professional: how Brazilians achieved eSports success in counter-strike: global offensive. In J. Hiltscher & T. M. Scholz (Eds.), *eSports yearbook 2017/18* (pp. 121–140). Norderstedt: Books on Demand GmbH.

Mooney, C. (2018). *Inside the E-Sports industry.* North Mankato, MN: Norwood House Press.

Newman, J. (2008). *Playing with videogames.* Abingdon: Routledge.

Newzoo. (2020a). Key numbers. Retrieved 13 July, 2020, from https://newzoo.com/key-numbers/

Newzoo. (2020b). Most viewed games. Retrieved 28 January, 2020, from https://platform.newzoo.com/rankings/streaming

Nielsen Esports. (2017). *The Esports playbook: maximizing your investment through understanding the fans.* N. Pike & S. Master (Eds.). Retrieved from http://www.nielsen.com/us/en/insights/reports/2017/the-esports-playbook-maximizing-investment-through-understanding-the-fans.html

Owens, M. D. (2016). What's in a name? eSports, betting, and gaming law. *Gaming Law Review and Economics*, *20*(7), 567–570. https://doi.org/10.1089/glre.2016.2075

Pannekeet, J. (2019, February 12). Newzoo: global Esports economy will top $1 billion for the first time in 2019. Retrieved 14 July, 2020, from https://newzoo.com/insights/articles/newzoo-global-esports-economy-will-top-1-billion-for-the-first-time-in-2019/

Parkin, S. (2015). *Death by video game: tales of obsession from the virtual frontline*. London: Serpent's Tail.

Peša, A. R., Čičin-Šain, D., & Blažević, T. (2017). New business model in the growing e-sports industry. *Poslovna izvrsnost: znanstveni časopis za promicanje kulture kvalitete i poslovne izvrsnosti*, *11*(2), 121–131. https://doi.org/10.22598/pi-be/2017.11.2.121

Scholz, C. (2010a). Gamers as a safety hazard. In J. Christophers & T. Scholz (Eds.), *eSports yearbook 2009* (pp. 51–52). Norderstedt: Books on Demand GmbH. Retrieved from http://esportsyearbook.com/eyb2009_ebook.pdf

Scholz, T. (2010b). eSports in the working world. In J. Christophers & T. Scholz (Eds.), *eSports yearbook 2009* (pp. 57–58). Norderstedt: Books on Demand GmbH. Retrieved from http://esportsyearbook.com/eyb2009_ebook.pdf

Şentuna, B., & Kanbur, D. (2016). What kind of an activity is a virtual game? A postmodern approach in relation to concept of phantasm by Deleuze and the philosophy of Huizinga. *Sport, Ethics and Philosophy*, *10*(1), 42–50. https://doi.org/10.1080/17511321.2016.1177581

Shabir, N. (2017). *Esports: the complete guide 17/18: a guide for gamers, teams, organisations and other entities in, or looking to get into the space*. Wroclaw: Independently Published.

Statista. (2018, January). Number of unique viewers of selected eSports tournaments worldwide from 2012 to 2017 (in millions). Retrieved 16 March, 2018, from https://www.statista.com/statistics/507491/esports-tournaments-by-number-viewers-global/

Statista. (2020, April). eSports audience size worldwide from 2018 to 2023, by type of viewers. Retrieved 13 July, 2020, from https://www.statista.com/statistics/490480/global-esports-audience-size-viewer-type/

Stein, V., & Scholz, T. M. (2016). Sky is the limit – Esports as entrepreneurial innovator for media management. In S. N. d. Jesus & P. Pinto (Eds.), *Proceedings of the International Congress on Interdisciplinarity in Social and Human Sciences* (pp. 622–631). Faro: University of Algarve. CIEO—Research Centre for Spatial and Organizational Dynamics. Retrieved from http://hdl.handle.net/10400.1/9888

Stivers, C. (2017). The first competitive video gaming anti-doping policy and its deficiencies under European Union law. *San Diego International Law Journal*, *18*(2), 263–294. Retrieved from http://digital.sandiego.edu/ilj/vol18/iss2/4/

Ströh, J. H. A. (2017). *The eSports market and eSports sponsoring*. Marburg: Tectum Verlag.

SuperData. (2017a, December). Esports courtside: playmakers of 2017. Retrieved 6 April, 2018, from http://strivesponsorship.com/wp-content/uploads/2017/12/SuperData-2017-Esports-Market-Brief.pdf

SuperData. (2017b, February). European eSports conference brief. Retrieved 6 April, 2018, from http://strivesponsorship.com/wp-content/uploads/2017/04/Superdata-2017-esports-market-brief.pdf

Sylvester, R., & Rennie, P. (2017). The world's fastest-growing sport: maximizing the economic success of esports whilst balancing regulatory concerns and ensuring the protection of those involved. *Gaming Law Review, 21*(8), 625–629. https://doi.org/10.1089/glr2.2017.21811

Tavinor, G. (2009). *The art of videogames*. Malden, MA: John Wiley & Sons.

Taylor, T. L. (2012). *Raising the Stakes: E-Sports and the professionalization of computer gaming*. Cambridge: The MIT Press.

Teichert, T., Gainsbury, S. M., & Mühlbach, C. (2017). Positioning of online gambling and gaming products from a consumer perspective: a blurring of perceived boundaries. *Computers in Human Behavior, 75*, 757–765. http://doi.org/10.1016/j.chb.2017.06.025

Wilson, J. L. (2017, June 5). How I learned to stop hating and love Esports. Retrieved 10 June, 2018, from https://www.pcmag.com/article/354028/how-i-learned-to-stop-hating-and-love-esports

Winnan, C. D. (2016). *An entrepreneur's guide to the exploding world of eSports: understanding the commercial significance of counter-strike, league of legends and DotA 2*. Kindle eBook: The Borderland Press.

Zolides, A. (2015). Lipstick bullets: labour and gender in professional gamer self-branding. *Persona Studies, 1*(2), 42–53. https://doi.org/10.21153/ps2015vol1no2art467

7 Communication Experts' Perspective on Esports

Angel Torres-Toukoumidis, Isidro Marín-Gutiérrez, and Mari Carmen Caldeiro Pedreira

Introduction

Esports have permeated different disciplines and fields of study, especially computer science (Qian, 2021), business administration (Radman Peša et al., 2017), physical education (Viscione & D'Elia, 2019), language learning (Fuentes & Navas, 2020a), psychology (Leung et al., 2021), law (Burk, 2013), gender studies (Groen, 2016), among others. However, one of the academic bases that has promoted the analysis and development of Esports has been the communication sciences, positioning the scientific contributions of this phenomenon in the academic world (Sell, 2015).

In fact, reviewing the connection between communication studies and Esports at Scopus and Web of Science, the most relevant scientific databases in the world, several common patterns are observed such as that the maximum number of authors are affiliated to Finnish universities, Tampere University and the University of Turku; the authors with most publications in five years have been Juho Hamari, Max Sjöblom and Joseph Macey, who belong to the universities mentioned above; for their part, the most productive year of these publications was 2020 with approximately 35 publications on this subject. Finally, the publisher with the greatest follow-up in the field of Esports has been Taylor and Francis with 28 publications. In short, this opens the discussion on whether this is a temporary trend in which academic experts in the communication area see this time as an opportunity for publishing in an ephemeral context and with an expiry date, or, on the contrary, it is a phenomenon that will be constantly evolving and will act as one of the main fields of media entertainment.

The contributions from the communication field to Esports have demonstrated their involvement by covering multiple lines of research, including audiovisual strategies (Taylor, 2016), media (Rodríguez,

DOI: 10.4324/9781003273691-10

2019), advertising (Byun & Kim, 2020; Fanjul-Peyro et al., 2019), narratives (Xue et al., 2019; Muñoz & Esteban, 2021), speech and linguistics (Boguslavskaya et al., 2020). The followings are some of these contributions:

- Qian et al. (2020) estimate that the relationship with the media and content industry has added several factors that increase the interest of Esports viewers, including virtual rewards, chat rooms, characteristics of casters and quality of transmission. The latter is a major factor for Esports competitions, so much so that the broadcast at mass levels together with the journalistic broadcast of these recreational activities has resulted in the games changing their esthetics adapted to the "Western" player, demanding a change of perception dependent on the trends shown by the media (Johnson & Woodcock, 2017).
- The rapid growth of Esports in the new digital media has meant that millions of people watch the broadcasts being attracted by the naturalness, spontaneity, knowledge and novelty of their players (Hamari & Sjöblom, 2017), i.e., beyond the game, viewers are captivated by the actions of the participants during the competitions and not directly by the videogame.
- Another of the spaces where Esports have been imbued are traditional sports, spaces with a linear attachment to the media. According to Finn (2020), the media coverage of traditional sports through Esports has attracted new fans and resulted in the development of new skills, which also occurred with motorsports. Also, concerning sports marketing and branding, Esports do not destabilize or reinforce the identity of the sports club among its fans, but they simply change the offer of a brand (Mühlbacher et al., 2021).

Finally, in addition to the contributions mentioned such as the extra value of the interfaces common to communication, the inclination of the players and the attachment to traditional sports demonstrated during the Covid-19 pandemic, the cancellation and postponement of sport events showed an opportunity for new media production to expand content dissemination strategies that included the use of streaming platforms with Esports and a professional moment for young people (Goldman & Hedlund, 2020). In assessing this context, what is ultimately the relation between Esports and communication? How do communication experts perceive this media phenomenon? Indeed, these questions, still unresolved from academia, are intended to be addressed in this research, analyzing the theoretical and technical contributions of competitions to the media.

Methodology

The aim of this research is to analyze the relation between Esports and the media. Thus, the specific objective is to examine the perception of communication experts regarding the contributions of Esports in aspects related to transmission, narration, professionalism, journalistic genres, roles of journalists, vocabulary, content, dissemination and learning.

The research has a descriptive qualitative design, defined as the processing of data and properties of a social phenomenon with the purpose of determining situations and patterns in the data (Lahitte & Sánchez Vázquez, 2013). To this end, 20 semi-structured interviews were conducted with communication experts from Europe and Latin America. For the selection of experts, profiles were reviewed through a non-probabilistic sampling with at least ten years of experience in higher education, in the field of communication and new technologies coming from institutions of the following countries: Ecuador, Venezuela, Mexico, Chile, Colombia, Argentina, Portugal and Spain; the experts who participated belong to the Salesian Polytechnic University (Ecuador), the Private Technical University of Loja (Ecuador), the University of Cuenca (Ecuador), the Technical University of the North (Ecuador), the Autonomous University of Chihuahua (Mexico), FLACSO (Mexico and Ecuador), Silva Henriquez University (Chile), the University of Playa Ancha (Chile), Universidad Metropolitana (Venezuela), Universidad Católica Andrés Bello (Venezuela), Universidad Santa María (Venezuela), the University of Valle (Colombia), the University of Rosario (Colombia), the University of Palermo (Argentina), Universidade Beira Interior (Portugal), the University of Seville (Spain), the University of Santiago de Compostela (Spain) and the University of La Laguna (Spain).

The interview had ten questions adapted from the indicators presented by Fuentes and Navas (2020b), Rodas Noguera (2021), Martín Muñoz and Pedrero Esteban (2021), Gallego Acosta (2019) organized in two sections in which two explanatory videos were used as support material to the experts. The first section refers to general questions about Esports and communication composed of four questions about their perspective toward this social phenomenon, its role with traditional media, digital and streaming platforms. The second set of questions has been called "specific questions about Esports and communication" composed of six questions concerning narration, vocabulary, technical professionalism, pre-production, assembly, production, post-production, journalistic genres, the work of commentators, financing and the notion of communicative education.

The questions were applied using Google Forms from October 8, 2021, to December 20, 2021, and were coded descriptively by identifying the topic covered and systematizing the answers provided by the experts using the software Voyant Tools, databasic.io and Atlas.ti v.9. The information obtained is presented below.

Results

It is important to mention that 18/20 (90%) of respondents have a favorable outlook on Esports, mainly because they see Esports as part of the digitized society that integrates with new technology as an alternative for networked entertainment, being an innovative space to learn new digital skills that promote new behaviors and new ways of living together. Figure 7.1 shows some of the most common used words.

Regarding the role of traditional media, digital media and streaming platforms, it is known that traditional media will have a passive role in providing visibility to news and reports which will progressively adapt to the broadcast of these events with a professional coverage, acting as promoters and future sponsors as happens in Spain with *As* newspaper (https://esports.as.com/) and Movistar channel https://ubeat.tv.

Figure 7.1 Why do most consider the emergence of Esports as positive?
Source: Own elaboration

In contrast, digital media will take an active, professional, primary and dominant role in Esports by integrating them into the broadcasts, enabling the consolidation of audiovisual resources, involving them in specialized programs and establishing revenues in the broadcast. Some of the phrases submitted by the experts were:

They will look for options and mechanisms to integrate them into their broadcasts. I think a symbiosis of digital infotainment will be experienced.

The creation of an Esports-specific section

Although streaming, Twitch and YouTube will play a central role by formalizing the growth of Esports seen in the reach, diversity, easy access and positioning, several of the experts mention that Netflix and Facebook projects prospect the transmission of live competitions of Esports with metaverse.

Regarding specific questions, the relation of Esports with the narration and vocabulary of the commentators, technical professionalism of pre-production, assembly, production and post-production, journalistic genres, journalistic works, funding and type of education related to media literacy was taken into account.

In relation to the narration, a positive estimate is observed in the commentators of these competitions, specifically when mentioning new profiles for the sports narrative specialized in tournaments, rules, tactics and strategies with a non-professional voice that narrates the events that seek to be transmitted with energy, emotion, power and rhythm. Similarly, the appropriateness of the language at the Esports events is asked based on this question, where most experts concentrate on two issues; the first one refers to emotionality and passion, falling into informality which is an attractive aspect for the public. The second question concerns game-specific technicalities expressed through a variety of anglicisms for a specialist audience on the subject. In other words, these events combine colloquial and everyday language with terms that are consubstantial to video games.

Considering the technical professionalism of pre-production, assembly, production and post-production, a fairly high level is prescribed at the audiovisual level with a high-quality management and a high investment. Experts demonstrate that transmissions tend to be linear, lacking depth and image interleaving; therefore, they recommend that it can be optimized with a 4D system, slow motion, use of different camera angles and associated resources, providing a much more colorful and dynamic broadcast.

Complementing this idea, experts examine the journalistic genres that could be coupled with these kinds of events in which, although it mentioned the incorporation of journalistic chronicles that consists of the orderly and detailed narration of a series of events from beginning to end, news is also suggested for competency results, interviews for featured participants and reports to broadcast in-depth explanations. They also consider that genres can classify journalistic styles, while the notion of formats could be added. They provide a more interactive space which leads to greater user participation through live streaming and coral interviews.

In another significant finding of the study, there are heterogeneous subjects who can exercise journalistic works at the Esports events such as ex-players, players, experts and journalists. Balanced groups should be made where the journalist guides the interaction by diversifying collaborations with multidisciplinary teams. These teams must provide dynamic narration combined with knowledge of Esports. In short, Figure 7.2 demonstrates the most common profiles in Esports events

Regarding financing, communication experts responded thoroughly, saying that resources can originate from a series of business models ranging from total sponsorship to hypersegmentation of income with support from the technology industry, the entertainment industry

Figure 7.2 Who do you think should perform journalistic works during Esport events?

and the video game industry. In the field of communication, there are different financing options:

- Broadcasting rights granted to television companies and streaming platforms.
- Broadcasting rights.
- Subscription and content memberships, also known as micropayments by Pay Per View (Arjona & Muñoz, 2020).
- Sports Team Sponsorship.
- Direct advertising. It is observed in brands.
- Indirect advertising. Monetization from clicks.

There is great openness to new business models in Esports, especially when the services offered combine both conventional and non-conventional strategies, thus extending the magnitude of these events.

Finally, Esports also provide teaching related to the educommunication and media environment. However, experts are wary of their responses as they consider Esports to be an emerging space where it would be difficult to objectively assess the effectiveness of short-, medium- and long-term learning. In short, it can be seen that Esports are a type of informal learning aimed at interconnectivity in which participants are taught in digital, hypermedia and locutionary competencies. They also take into account that it promotes immersion into new cultures and languages.

Conclusions

The media breadth produced by Esports has interested communication professionals by demonstrating that this phenomenon is present and that the experiences could modify the interactive activities in new generations by articulating new participation thresholds. In other words, to understand Esports it is necessary to assimilate the new information and communication channels used by young people.

In summary, experts mention that traditional media will adapt to transmission as future sponsors, while the role of digital media will be considered for Esports, relating it with streaming platforms through accessibility, diversity and positioning.

Another characteristic observed in these events is related with the technical aspects: narrators normally combine informal language with specialized language, favoring the incorporation of new technological systems like 4D, integration of rigid multidisciplinary teams by professional communicators, players and former players, multiple millionaire industries, entertainment, computing and communication that guarantee a successful future.

In short, it is uncertain if the communication experts' perspective on the future of the Esports is apt; however, they have certainly changed the digital world by building a new information paradigm.

References

Arjona, J., & Muñoz, V. (2020). La consolidación del modelo game-as-a-service en la industria del videojuego. Micropagos, cajas botín y su problemática legal. *Revista Inclusiones, 7*, 229–244.

Boguslavskaya, V., Sharakhina, L. V., & Tomaščíková, S. (2020). Visualisation of digital media discourses: a case study of Russian language esports media. *SKASE Journal of Theoretical Linguistics, 17*(5), 192–201.

Burk, D. L. (2013). Owning e-Sports: proprietary rights in professional computer gaming. *University of Pennsylvania Law Review, 161*(6), 1535–1578.

Byun, K. W., & Kim, S. (2020). A study on the effects of advertising attributes in YouTube e-sport video. *International Journal of Internet, Broadcasting and Communication, 12*(2), 137–143.

Fanjul-Peyro, C., Gonzalez-Onate, C., & Pena-Hernandez, P. J. (2019). eGamers' influence in brand advertising strategies. A comparative study between Spain and Korea. *Comunicar. Media Education Research Journal, 27*(1), 105–113.

Finn, M. (2020). From accelerated advertising to Fanboost: mediatized motorsport. *Sport in Society, 24*(6), 937–953. https://doi.org/10.1080/17430437.2019.1710131

Fuentes, A. Y. P., & Navas, M. F. (2020a). El aprendizaje de lenguas extranjeras en los e-sports: una revisión teórica. *Magister, 9*–15.

Fuentes, A. Y. P., & Navas, M. F. (2020b). Factors influencing foreign language learning in eSports. A case study. *Qualitative Research in Education, 9*(2), 128–159.

Gallego Acosta, P. J. (2019). *E-sports, orígenes y oportunidades de negocio.* [Tesis de Licenciatura]. Universidad Politécnica de Cartagena.

Goldman, M. M., & Hedlund, D. P. (2020). Rebooting content: broadcasting sport and esports to homes during COVID-19. *International Journal of Sport Communication, 13*(3), 370–380.

Groen, M. (2016). (Un) doing gender?: Female tournaments in the e-sports scene. *International Journal of Gaming and Computer-Mediated Simulations (IJGCMS), 8*(4), 25–37.

Hamari, J., & Sjöblom, M. (2017). What is eSports and why do people watch it?. *Internet Research, 27*(2), 211–232.

Johnson, M. R., & Woodcock, J. (2017). Fighting games and go: exploring the aesthetics of play in professional gaming. *Thesis Eleven, 138*(1), 26–45.

Lahitte, H. B., & Sánchez Vázquez, M. J. (2013). Tratamiento de resultados en diseños cualitativos: La aplicación del Análisis Descriptivo. *Revista Latinoamericana de Metodología de las Ciencias Sociales, 3*(2), 1–12.

Leung, K. M., Wong, M. Y. C., Ou, K. L., Chung, P. K., & Lau, K. L. (2021). Assessing Esports participation intention: the development and psychometric properties of the theory of planned behavior-based Esports Intention Questionnaire (TPB-Esport-Q). *International Journal of Environmental Research and Public Health, 18*(23), 12653.

Mühlbacher, H., Bertschy, M., & Desbordes, M. (2021). Brand identity dynamics–reinforcement or destabilisation of a sport brand identity through the introduction of esports?. *Journal of Strategic Marketing*, 1–22. https://www.tandfonline.com/doi/abs/10.1080/0965254X.2021.1959628?journalCode=rjsm20

Muñoz, D. M., & Esteban, L. M. P. (2021). Deporte y espectáculo en la narrativa de los 'e-sports': El caso de 'League of legends'. Index. comunicación: *Revista científica en el ámbito de la Comunicación Aplicada, 11*(2), 59–79.

Qian, F. (2021). Simulation training of E-Sports players based on wireless sensor network. *Wireless Communications and Mobile Computing*. https://search.crossref.org/?q=10.1155%2F2021%2F9636951&from_ui=yes#

Qian, T. Y., Zhang, J. J., Wang, J. J., & Hulland, J. (2020). Beyond the game: dimensions of esports online spectator demand. *Communication & Sport, 8*(6), 825–851.

Radman Peša, A., Čičin-Šain, D., & Blažević, T. (2017). New business model in the growing e-sports industry. *Poslovna izvrsnost, 11*(2), 121–131.

Rodas Noguera, D. (2021). *El tratamiento informativo de los eSports en los medios de comunicación en España: El caso de El Desmarque, VANDAL El Español, ABC y El País.* [Tesis de Licenciatura]. Universidad de Sevilla.

Rodríguez, A. P. (2019). e-Sports y medios de comunicación. *Creatividad y sociedad: revista de la Asociación para la Creatividad, 30*, 75–103.

Sell, J. J. C. (2015). *E-Sports broadcasting* [Doctoral dissertation, Massachusetts Institute of Technology]. https://dspace.mit.edu/bitstream/handle/1721.1/97996/914473590-MIT.pdf?sequence=1&isAllowed=y

Taylor, N. (2016). Play to the camera: video ethnography, spectatorship, and e-sports. *Convergence, 22*(2), 115–130.

Viscione, I., & D'Elia, F. (2019). Augmented reality for learning in distance education: the case of e-sports. *Journal of Physical Education and Sport, 19*, 2047–2050.

Xue, H., Newman, J. I., & Du, J. (2019). Narratives, identity and community in esports. *Leisure Studies, 38*(6), 845–861.

Index